Cambridge Elements

Elements in Epistemology
edited by
Stephen Hetherington
University of New South Wales, Sydney

SINCERITY AND INSINCERITY

Neri Marsili
University of Turin

CAMBRIDGE
UNIVERSITY PRESS

Shaftesbury Road, Cambridge CB2 8EA, United Kingdom

One Liberty Plaza, 20th Floor, New York, NY 10006, USA

477 Williamstown Road, Port Melbourne, VIC 3207, Australia

314–321, 3rd Floor, Plot 3, Splendor Forum, Jasola District Centre,
New Delhi – 110025, India

Cambridge University Press is part of Cambridge University Press & Assessment,
a department of the University of Cambridge.

We share the University's mission to contribute to society through the pursuit of
education, learning and research at the highest international levels of excellence.

www.cambridge.org
Information on this title: www.cambridge.org/9781009671033

DOI: 10.1017/9781009348683

First published 2026

A catalogue record for this publication is available from the British Library

*A Cataloging-in-Publication data record for this Element is available
from the Library of Congress*

ISBN 978-1-009-67103-3 Hardback
ISBN 978-1-009-34869-0 Paperback
ISSN 2398-0567 (online)
ISSN 2514-3832 (print)

Sincerity and Insincerity

Elements in Epistemology

DOI: 10.1017/9781009348683
First published online: April 2026

Neri Marsili
University of Turin

Author for correspondence: Neri Marsili, neri.marsili@unito.it

Abstract: Sincerity is essential to communication: without a norm of sincerity, we could hardly trust what other people tell us. But what does it take to be sincere, exactly? And why is sincerity so important? *Sincerity and Insincerity* offers a comprehensive review of existing philosophical work on the nature of sincerity and its epistemic value. It puts forward a novel, fine-grained account of what sincerity and insincerity are, and explores into the grey area between the two, identifying various ways in which speakers can be partially sincere. Integrating ideas from different philosophical subfields and traditions, it offers an updated perspective on what makes sincerity epistemically valuable, giving serious consideration to the idea that sincerity is the norm of assertion. Overall, this Element provides a novel, informed perspective on what sincerity is, how it works, and why it matters.

Keywords: sincerity, norm of assertion, speech act theory, testimony, communication

ISBNs: 9781009671033 (HB), 9781009348690 (PB), 9781009348683 (OC)
ISSNs: 2398-0567 (online), 2514-3832 (print)

Contents

1 Introduction

> *[The study of communication] is in principle the [study of] everything which can be used in order to lie. If something cannot be used to tell a lie, conversely it cannot be used to tell the truth: it cannot in fact be used 'to tell' at all.*
>
> Umberto Eco, *A Theory of Semiotics*

Communication is fundamental to our lives – arguably, it is one of the things that make us distinctively human. Our ability to communicate, however, comes at a price: by allowing us to exchange information, it makes us equally vulnerable to misinformation. Communication, then, is a double-edged sword: the ability to communicate sincerely is essentially entangled with the ability to communicate insincerely. The purpose of this Element is to explore these two sides of communication: sincerity and insincerity.

We will begin by tackling definitional questions. What is sincerity, and what is insincerity? How do they differ from related concepts, like veracity, omission, deception, or lying? These questions have preoccupied philosophers since ancient times. Nowadays, two main paradigms dominate the theoretical landscape. Speaker-centred views (Section 2.2) conceive of sincerity as a match (and insincerity as a mismatch) between what the speaker believes and what they claim. Hearer-centred views (Section 2.3) focus instead on the intended effect on the hearer (to inform or to misinform). After introducing these views, we'll see how they can be progressively refined to tackle complications of increasing complexity, such as graded beliefs, non-literal communication, and non-assertoric speech (Sections 2.4–2.7).

The second half of this Element (Section 3) applies this conceptual toolbox to the normative dimension of sincerity. Many philosophers consider sincerity to be an extremely important virtue, and insincerity an unforgivable vice. For some 'absolutist' thinkers like Augustine and Kant, no circumstances can ever justify being insincere – not even saving a life. But why do philosophers deem sincerity so important? After examining the norm of sincerity (Section 3.1), and its interaction with other norms (Section 3.2), we'll consider what it means to understand sincerity as a virtue (Section 3.3), and explore what makes sincerity so valuable across different linguistic communities.

The Element concludes by examining sincerity's role in sustaining communication, social cooperation, and knowledge transmission (Section 3.4), with particular emphasis on its epistemic value (Section 3.5). Contemporary philosophers often argue that testimony is governed by epistemic expectations that exceed sincerity – such as the 'knowledge-norm', which demands that one should assert only what one knows. Against this background, we'll consider some arguments in favour of a once-popular idea that has recently fallen out of fashion: the view that sincerity is all that assertion demands. Before we can get there, though, we have to ask a more fundamental question: what is sincerity, exactly?

2 What Is Sincerity?

In 1972, operatives connected to Richard Nixon's re-election campaign broke into the Democratic National Committee headquarters at the Watergate complex in Washington DC, to wiretap phones and photograph campaign documents. Nixon repeatedly denied involvement or knowledge of the break-in, including in a televised address to the nation in 1973, in which he stated:

(1)   I had no prior knowledge of the Watergate break-in; I neither took part in nor knew about any of the subsequent cover-up activities.

Nixon's denials were soon proven untruthful, when Oval Office tapes revealed his direct involvement in the cover-up. These revelations eventually led to his resignation on 9 August 1974, to avoid impeachment.

Nixon's statement is a paradigmatic case of insincerity: (1) was a believed-false statement, uttered with the intention of deceiving its recipients. Paradigmatic cases of sincerity, by contrast, involve stating what you believe to be true, with the intention of passing that information on to your audience. Unlike insincere statements like (1), sincere statements rarely make for great stories: since sincerity is the rule, the fact that someone chose to speak sincerely is typically uneventful.

The adjectives 'sincere' and 'insincere' can be used in at least two senses. Sometimes they are used to describe *a property of utterances* – that is, of communicative acts made in a certain context. I may say, for example, that (1) was 'insincere' because, in uttering (1), Nixon intentionally misrepresented his involvement in the Watergate break-in. In this sense, insincerity is predicated of a particular utterance, relative to a particular agent (the speaker) and a particular context. I will call this conception, which focuses on the sincerity of specific utterances, 'sincerity in discourse' (or 'discursive sincerity'[1]), and it will be the main concern of this Element.

On the other hand, ascriptions of sincerity and insincerity are sometimes focused on the speaker, rather than the utterance. I may say, for example, that Nixon was an insincere politician, and that (1) was definitely in character. When 'sincere' and 'insincere' are used in this way, they refer to *dispositions* or *character traits* – they describe what a certain person tends to do under certain

---

[1] 'Discourse' here stands for communication in general. It's less precise, but makes for a slightly more readable label.

circumstances (a disposition) or the psychological features that underlie these dispositions (a character trait). I will call this the '*dispositional*' conception of sincerity and insincerity. While I'll occasionally touch upon it (Section 3.3), it will not be the main concern of this Element.

The contrast between dispositional and discursive conceptions of sincerity is lexicalised in our vocabulary for lying. We distinguish between a *liar* (someone who has a disposition to lie) and a *lie* (an insincere utterance). English doesn't offer comparable lexicalised entries for sincerity and insincerity. Sure, we can distinguish between an *insincere statement* (close, but not equivalent, to the notion of a lie) and an *insincere speaker* (close, but not equivalent, to the notion of a liar). But even these compound constructions maintain some ambiguity: ascribed to a speaker, insincerity can refer both to a speaker's disposition in general (e.g. 'Nixon was an insincere politician') and to a speaker's communicative act (e.g. 'Nixon was insincere *in stating (1)*'). To disambiguate, I will therefore distinguish between *discursive* and *dispositional* conceptions of sincerity.

2.1 Sincerity in Discourse and Beyond

2.1.1 Communication: A Precondition for Sincerity

There is a prejudice against the spoken lie, but none against any other, and by examination and mathematical computation I find that the proportion of the spoken lie to the other varieties is as 1 to 22,894. Therefore the spoken lie is of no consequence, and it is not worth while to go around fussing about it and trying to make believe that it is an important matter.

Mark Twain, My First Lie, and How I Got Out of It

In *Parerga e Paralipomena*, Arthur Schopenhauer writes that 'there is in the world only one mendacious and hypocritical being, namely man. Every other is true and sincere, in that it frankly and openly declares itself to be what it is and expresses itself as it feels'. Unlike animals, whose ingenuity and transparency are fascinating to us, the degenerate human tendency to lie 'stands as a blot on Nature'.

Schopenhauer's harsh comments are comically inaccurate: plants and animals are capable of incredibly creative and complex forms of deception. However, there's a grain of truth in his observation: although many non-human organisms are able to deceive, there's a sense in which lying and insincerity (unlike deceiving) are exclusive to the domain of coded, linguistic communication – that is, to human communication.

Take the orchid *Cryptostylis erecta*, which is pollinated by the so-called orchid dupe wasp (*Lissopimpla excelsa*). Male wasps mistake the orchid for female wasps, and copulate with them. While there is a sense in which the wasp is deceived by the orchid's shape, it would be a stretch to say that the orchid *lied* to the wasp, or that the orchid was *insincere*. Instead, it seems appropriate to distinguish between the broader concept of *deception* and the narrower concept of *insincerity*. Anything designed[2] to induce false representations of the world (even an orchid's appearance) can be deemed deceptive. Insincerity, as I'll understand it, is instead a property of communicative acts. This also rules out human deception that doesn't rely on communication, whose best illustration is perhaps offered by Kant's (LE) example of a person who ostentatiously prepares their suitcases to persuade a friend that they are about to leave for a long trip.

The idea that insincerity requires linguistic communication can be traced back to Augustine (*Contra Mendacio* XII), who wrote that 'a lie is a false signification by words'. Aquinas (ST, q110) clarifies that 'words' should be understood in a loose sense:

> *When it is said that 'a lie is a false signification by words,' the term 'words' denotes every kind of sign. Wherefore if a person intended to signify something false by means of signs, he would not be excused from lying.*

Indeed, we can communicate insincerely without using words, by using any sort of conventional signals. I might nod my head to insincerely express agreement (even if I disagree), or I might send insincere messages by using other non-verbal conventional codes, like smoke signals, Morse code, maritime flag signals, and so forth.

Sensu stricto, then, sincerity and insincerity are properties of communicative acts – specifically, they belong to the realm of conventional, intentional communication. I won't attempt to characterise these notions too precisely (although I'll draw some boundaries in the sections that follow), as it would lead us astray. For current purposes, it's enough to have established a first intuitive distinction between non-verbal deception (illustrated by Kant's suitcase packer and the misleading orchids) and insincere discourse. The following sections will refine this distinction.

2.1.2 Omission

Ricky Gervais's movie *The Invention of Lying* imagines a world in which lying has not been invented yet: everybody is sincere all the time. Not only do the characters say only what they believe to be true: they seem unable to withhold information that we would typically keep to ourselves (embarrassing details,

---

[2] What exactly qualifies as a deceptive evolutionary 'design' is discussed in animal signalling studies (e.g. Smith and Harper 2003; Searcy and Nowicki 2005) and in the philosophy of deception (e.g. Artiga and Paternotte 2018; Fallis and Lewis 2021).

sexual desires, etc.). In a scene, for example, a waiter welcomes a couple by disclosing irrelevant personal information: 'I'm very embarrassed to work here. And [to the woman] you're very pretty'.

The movie implicitly assumes that omitting information amounts to lying. While this assumption yields good comedic effects, it also engenders conceptual confusion. We saw that lying rather requires communicating something. By refraining from communicating, then, one cannot lie. Similarly, if we understand insincerity as a property of communicative acts, failing to disclose information won't qualify as insincerity either.

This is not to say that *no* act of omission ever deserves to be called insincere. In some circumstances, by staying silent a speaker can communicate a specific proposition. For example, an informer wearing a wire might be instructed 'Cough if the mafia boss is there, otherwise stay silent'. Here a message can be sent by remaining in silence. Generalising, when there is an explicit mutual understanding that failing to speak amounts to communicating a specific proposition (e.g. 'The boss is not here') we have 'silent communication' (if we allow the oxymoron). Silent communication can be insincere, but is clearly different from withholding information: the former involves communicating something, while the latter does not (Mahon 2015).[3]

That noted, by failing to speak up, one can still be culpable of *deception by omission*, which is pro tanto morally objectionable. For example, I might resent a friend for keeping me in the dark about my partner's love affairs, or a colleague for not warning me that they accidentally spilt coffee on my laptop while I was on my lunch break. In such cases, however, failing to disclose some content p doesn't amount to communicating that p is false – at most, it is to let someone *infer* that p is false. It would, therefore, not be insincerity sensu stricto, since no communicative act is involved.

While deceptive omissions fall out of the scope of 'discursive insincerity', there's admittedly *some* sense in which they can be insincere. The characters in *The Invention of Lying*, who disclose all information that they deem relevant to the conversation, display a propensity to be transparent that closely resembles sincerity, despite exceeding its demands. I will call them 'supersincere' to indicate that, on top of saying only what they believe, they also disclose all information that they deem relevant to the audience. Supersincerity sometimes clashes with other social norms (such as politeness and privacy, cf. Section 3.2): that's why Gervais's movie characters, who can't help violating such norms, come across as awkward and comical.

---

[3] Recent philosophical work has explored additional ways in which conversational silences can function as genuine communicative acts (Goldberg 2020; Klieber 2024). For broader discussion of omission in relation to deception, see Nagel 1998, Fallis 2018, Heffer 2020, and Section 2.4.

2.1.3 Sincerity beyond Communication

I sincerely believe that banking establishments are more dangerous than standing armies

Thomas Jefferson

In ordinary language, sincerity is sometimes ascribed beyond the realm of communication. Actions can be described as sincere and insincere: we speak of a sincere kiss, or a sincere attempt to help. Beliefs, too, admit such descriptions, like Jefferson's 'sincere belief' that banking establishments are more dangerous than standing armies. Even a philosophical doctrine can be described as sincere or insincere. Writing about Schopenhauer's life, Bertrand Russell (1946, 726–27) notes:

> *[His] doctrine [was not] sincere, if we may judge by Schopenhauer's life. He habitually dined well, at a good restaurant; he had many trivial love-affairs, which were sensual but not passionate; he was exceedingly quarrelsome and unusually avaricious. On one occasion he was annoyed by an elderly seamstress who was talking to a friend outside the door of his apartment. He threw her downstairs, causing her permanent injury.*

What made Schopenhauer's doctrine 'insincere'? Presumably, a certain inconsistency between what Schopenhauer preached ('the virtue of asceticism and resignation'; 727) and his actions. When Russell wrote that Schopenhauer's philosophy was insincere, then, he meant that there was a 'mismatch' between what Schopenhauer preached and the way he acted. Both in discourse and beyond discourse, at the core of the notion of (in)sincerity there seems to be a contrast between two states: there's sincerity when there's a 'match' between two states, and insincerity when there is a mismatch or disconnect (Eriksson 2011).

In *discourse*, the contrast is between what one says and what one thinks: a sincere statement (assertion, claim)[4] is one that 'matches' one's beliefs. Sincerity in *action* can take a variety of forms. In Schopenhauer's case, the contrast is between what he preaches (his ascetic doctrine) and what he does (his indulgent lifestyle). But sincerity in action can also involve a contrast between one's actions and what one *believes* or feels – similarly to sincerity in discourse. A sincere kiss is one where the action (kissing) reflects my inner state (an emotion). A sincere attempt to help, an action that reflects a genuine will to be helpful. Whether the action is sincere here depends on whether you have the internal state that is supposed to accompany your act.

---

[4] Following an established tradition in speech act theory (see Searle and Vanderveken 1985, 183) I will use these terms ('statement', 'claim', and 'assertion') interchangeably to refer to speech acts that present their propositional content as true.

Sincerity in belief is more complex. When Jefferson claims that he 'sincerely believes' that banking establishments are dangerous, the expression is idiomatic: Jefferson actually means that he is making a sincere assertion (or that his belief is warranted and deeply held). But beliefs can also be described as 'insincere' in a more substantive sense. Paradigmatically, this happens when a believer is somewhat aware that their evidence doesn't support a given belief, but holds onto it nonetheless.

Suppose that Johnny firmly believes that he is a loving husband, despite being aware that he's culpable of all sorts of abuses. It might be said that Johnny's belief that he's a loving husband is 'insincere', because he clings on to this thought despite overwhelming evidence to the contrary. Once again, insincerity stems from a mismatch or disconnect: Johnny's awareness that his behaviour is abusive, and hence of what he should believe, doesn't match what he consciously believes.

Like sincerity in discourse, then, sincerity beyond discourse involves a mismatch or disconnect, typically between an internal representation of the world (a belief, desire, etc.) and some other representation (e.g. a representation in speech, in belief, or as expressed by an action).[5] Despite this connection with its non-verbal cognates, however, discursive sincerity constitutes a coherent, distinctive phenomenon that deserves treatment in its own right. I will therefore leave these related notions (*sincerity in action*, *sincerity in belief*, and *supersincerity*) behind, to better focus on sincerity in communication.

2.1.4 Falsity, Truth, and Veracity

It is 1 May 1486, in Córdoba, Spain. Christopher Columbus stands before Queen Isabella I and King Ferdinand II, presenting his ambitious plan. He declares:

(2)   Your Majesties, with a few ships we can reach the Indies by sailing west across the Atlantic Ocean, for about 750 leagues.

Famously, Columbus was wrong: he grossly miscalculated the distance between Spain and the Indies. Following his route, it would have taken approximately 3,500 leagues (about 20,000 km) to reach his destination. Columbus's statement was sincere,[6] but nonetheless false.

The example illustrates a familiar way in which sincerity and truth can come apart: honest mistakes. Our statements can fail to be true even if they are sincere: unfortunately, we humans aren't endowed with the gift of omniscience.

---

[5] Arguably, many of the examples discussed, such as behaving in ways that don't reflect our true nature and our deepest beliefs, are best described as failures of *authenticity*, rather than sincerity. For an introduction to the philosophy of authenticity, see Varga and Guignon 2023.

[6] In our imaginary example, that is. To avoid misunderstandings: there is no historical record of Columbus uttering this precise sentence (or its Castilian equivalent).

Sometimes we get things wrong; when we sincerely assert our wrong opinions, we make statements that are sincere but false.

The opposite can happen, although it's certainly a less familiar case: a statement can turn out to be true even if it's insincere. Consider the following example:

> CHEATING PLOT TWIST
> *Giacomo and Frida are married, but Giacomo is looking for an affair. At a party, he starts flirting with a woman called Ana. Ana knows that Giacomo is married. Hoping to make her feel comfortable about flirting with a married man, Giacomo tells her:*

(3)   *My wife has been cheating on me for the last few months.*

> *As it turns out, unbeknownst to Giacomo, Frida is really cheating on him.*

Giacomo is clearly insincere. But his statement turned out to be true: his wife is truly cheating on him. Just as sincerity is no guarantee of truth, insincerity is no guarantee of falsity.

The purpose of these examples is to impress upon the reader the important conceptual distinction between sincerity and veracity. Whether (2) and (3) are true or false doesn't depend on the speaker's subjective beliefs, but rather on *objective* features of the world[7] (whether the Indies are 750 leagues away; whether Frida is cheating on Giacomo). By contrast, whether (2) and (3) are sincere or insincere depends on the speaker's *subjective* mental states (did they believe that what they said was true? Were they aiming to deceive their interlocutor?). To stress the contrast between these two dimensions of evaluation, it will be useful to differentiate between veracity (the objective dimension of evaluation) and sincerity (the subjective dimension), and (correspondingly) between falsity and insincerity.

Armed with these conceptual distinctions, let's move on to analyse two main conceptions of sincerity: one that defines it as a relation between a speaker's statement and their mental states (the speaker-centred conception; Section 2.2), and one that defines it as a relation between their mental states and the mental states that they aim to induce in the hearer (the hearer-centred conception; Section 2.3).

2.2 The Expression View: Speaker-Centred Sincerity

> *Hateful in my eyes, even as the gates of Hades, is that man that hideth one thing in his chest and sayeth another.*
>
> Achilles, in the *Iliad, IX 312–31*

---

[7] All talk of objectivity is rejected by some philosophers. I will leave such controversies aside; see Williams 2002 (ch. 1) for discussion.

According to an influential philosophical view, communication is essentially a tool for self-expression – that is, for making public what's inside our minds. Without speech, every individual is an island. Our internal attitudes (beliefs, intentions, emotions) are private states inaccessible to others. The power of communication is that it allows us to make these states public: to *express* our mental states.

The idea that words are the outer expression of mental states can be traced back to Aristotle (*De Interpretatione*, § 1). It was later endorsed by Locke (1690, III, II, §1), and then revived and systematised in contemporary philosophy of language (Frege 1956; Searle 1979; Davis 2003; Green 2007). Unsurprisingly, the notion of attitude expression has been understood in slightly different ways by these authors. As I understand it, expressing a psychological state amounts to *representing oneself* as being in that psychological state. Put more bluntly: you express a mental state when you communicate that you have that mental state. For our purposes, I don't need to settle on a precise theory of thought-expression – that's for another book. But it's important to stress what expression, as it's understood here, *does not* involve.

First, expression is independent from persuasion (or even *attempted* persuasion).[8] When I say 'Ouch!' my cry expresses pain, regardless of whether I am attempting to convince you that I am in pain (my cry might be a mere reflex), and regardless of whether I succeed in convincing you that I am in pain. Second, since my focus is discursive insincerity, I will restrict my attention to expression achieved by means of linguistic, intentional communication. Third, *expressing* an attitude doesn't entail *having* that attitude:[9] my shouting 'Ouch!' can express pain regardless of whether I am, in fact, experiencing pain.

On this conception of communication, which I'll call the *expression view*, sincerity is deeply tied to thought expression. Expressing our private mental states opens up the possibility of misrepresentation. When there is a *match* between what the speaker claims and what they believe, their communicative act is sincere. When there is a mismatch instead, their assertion is insincere (Figure 1). Limiting our attention to assertoric, literal speech,[10] we can derive the following account of sincerity:

---

[8] In contrast with neo-Gricean accounts of expression, like Bach and Harnish's (1979), which require attempted persuasion as a necessary condition for expression.

[9] In contrast with authors who define expression in a way that requires having the corresponding mental state, like Davis (2003, 25), Green (2007a, 70–83), and Owens (2006).

[10] I will extend discussion to non-literal communication in Section 2.4, and to non-assertoric communication in Sections 2.7 and 3.2.

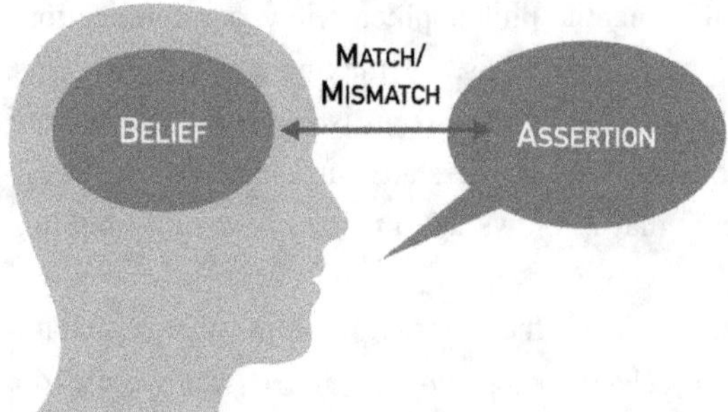

Figure 1 A visual representation of the standard expression view. Sincerity depends on whether the speaker believes or disbelieves the propositional content of their assertion.

STANDARD EXPRESSION
Sincerity depends on whether the speaker (S) expresses a content[11] that matches their actual beliefs.

- *An assertion is sincere iff S believes its content p to be true.*
- *An assertion is insincere iff S believes its content p to be false.*

This 'classical' or 'standard' conception of sincerity as a *match* between speech and thought (and insincerity as *mismatch)* finds resonance within a long philosophical tradition. In the fourth century, Augustine defined lying in terms of a *duplicity of the heart*[12] (*duplex cor*; DM, III, 3): '[The liar] has one thought hidden in his breast and another ready on his tongue, and this is the evil proper to the liar' (*Enquiridion, VI, 18*). The idea that lying consists in speaking in opposition to one's mind would subsequently become standard in medieval philosophy; following Raymond de Peñafort, Clem (2023) calls this the '*contra mentem*' (against the mind) principle.

2.2.1 Sincerely Asserting What You Believe to Be False

While STANDARD EXPRESSION works well for paradigmatic cases of sincerity and insincerity, it struggles to accommodate cases involving self-deception and fragmented beliefs.[13] To illustrate, consider the following scenario (from Ridge 2006; with edits):

---

[11] To simplify discussion, I'll use 'expressing a content/proposition' as a shorthand for 'expressing belief in a content/proposition'. When states other than belief are involved, I'll specify it explicitly.

[12] Griffiths 2004 elaborates this view.

[13] There's substantial scholarly debate on what self-deception is and how it works. For discussion, see Krstić (2025).

LOVELY MOTHER
Beppe believes that he believes his mother loves him, but deep down he actually doesn't believe that she does. In fact, Beppe believes his mother hates him. Beppe's behaviour betrays that he deludes himself about his own beliefs. For example, he might predict that his mother will do things that would make sense only if he believed she hated him. Beppe feels the sort of anxiety people associate with being hated by a close family member, goes out of his way to try to please her, is highly deferential to her, and so on. Nonetheless, because he cannot cope with the idea that his mother hates him, he has somehow convinced himself that he believes that she loves him. When we ask Beppe whether his mother loves him, he replies:

(4)   Yes, of course she does.

Beppe's assertion is intuitively sincere. After all, *he believes that he believes* (i.e. he has a 'higher order belief' – a belief about what he believes) that his mother loves him. However, what Beppe *really believes* (his first-order belief, independent of what he believes that he believes) is that his mother hates him. Interpreted literally, STANDARD EXPRESSION classifies (4) as *insincere*. Many scholars take this to be a problem (Ridge 2006, 488–89; Chan and Kahane 2011; Stokke 2018, 173–75).

As a solution, some suggest that the sincerity of an assertion depends on the conscious, higher-order mental states of the speaker, rather than their actual, deeply held beliefs (see e.g. Mellor 1977; Moran 2005).[14] On this view, sincerity is determined by the relationship between what someone says and their *higher-order beliefs* (their beliefs about what they believe):

HIGHER-ORDER EXPRESSION
Sincerity depends on whether the speaker (S) expresses a content that matches what they believe that they believe.

- *An assertion is sincere iff S believes that S believes its content to be true.*
- *An assertion is insincere iff S believes that S believes its content to be false.*

HIGHER-ORDER EXPRESSION gives the right verdict for cases of fragmented belief like LOVELY MOTHER. It judges Beppe to be sincere in asserting (4), even though Beppe actually believes that his mother hates him, because he *believes that he believes* that she loves him. Standard insincere statements like (1), too, are classified as insincere, since Nixon both believes that (1) is false and believes that it's false that he believes it. Nonetheless, even HIGHER-ORDER EXPRESSION faces some challenges.

---

[14] Higher-order beliefs and conscious beliefs can come apart under some circumstances. I'll ignore this complication here, as well as formulations in terms of *assent* (rather than belief), but see Stokke 2018 (177–80) for discussion.

2.2.2 Misspeaking and Intentions

How many animals of each kind did Moses take on the ark? If you are ready to answer 'Of course, Moses took two', you are in good company (Erickson and Mattson 1981). Yet, this isn't what you actually believe. You know that, according to the biblical myth, it was Noah, not Moses, who took animals on the ark. This common slip of tongue, known as the 'Moses Illusion', illustrates the concept of *misspeaking*: we sometimes try but fail to say what we want to say.

Those who misspeak are clearly not liars (Sorensen 2011). Sure, they fail to say what they believe. But accusations of mendacity aren't in order here. The victims of the Moses illusion might be distracted, but they are certainly not insincere. This yields a new problem for speaker-centred views. If you accidentally respond that Moses took two animals of each kind on the ark, you say something that you neither believe, nor believe that you believe. Every definition reviewed so far misclassifies misspeaking as insincere speech.

If this verdict is intuitively incorrect, it's arguably because misspeakers have no *intention* to misrepresent their beliefs. Perhaps, then, insincerity is a matter of communicating a proposition that *intentionally* misrepresents one's belief – and conversely, sincerity a matter of *intentionally* representing one's beliefs faithfully:

INTENTIONAL EXPRESSION
- *An assertion is sincere iff in making it, the speaker (S) intends to express a proposition that S believes to be true.*
- *An assertion is insincere iff in making it, S intends to express a proposition that S believes to be false.*[15]

There are notable precursors to this view. Augustine (DM) defined lying as an 'utterance accompanied by the intention to utter a falsehood'. Similarly, Aquinas (ST, II, II, 110) argued that 'the definition of lying is taken from formal falsity, i.e. from the fact that someone has the intention to state what is false'.[16] Many contemporary authors, too, have linked sincerity to an intention to communicate a proposition that matches one's beliefs (or fails to match, for insincerity).[17]

---

[15] Of course, for the assertion to be insincere, expressing a false proposition need not be the speaker's primary aim, nor an outcome desired for its own sake (Pepp 2018, 57-60; the reverse, of course, applies to sincerity). Accordingly, 'S intends to *f*' should be understood broadly: it covers not only S's ultimate goal, but also what S recognises as unavoidable in executing their plan for *f*-ing (cf. also Krstić 2023 on 'oblique intentions). On this understanding, *intending to tell you that I'm happy (when I know I'm not)* entails *intending to tell you something I disbelieve*, even if telling you something I disbelieve is not something I intend or desire to do for its own sake.

[16] These formulations require an intention to utter an *objective* falsehood, rather than a believed-false proposition. Still, any rational intention to utter a falsehood entails an intention to utter a believed-false proposition, hence the analogy with the intentional expression view.

[17] For Chan and Kahane (2011, 229), the speaker's dominant *motivation* determines sincerity. Fallis's (2012, 578) definition of lying closely aligns with Augustine and Aquinas. In previous

Of course, what matters for sincerity is the speaker's *conscious* intention. As I understand it, conscious intention is about having reflective access to the goals guiding one's action, rather than explicitly thinking about such goals. So, if I instinctively and spontaneously tell the truth, I am sincere, even if I have not explicitly thought 'I will now tell the truth' (Green 2007, 29; Stokke 2018, 181–86). I also understand intention to be constrained by what one thinks it's possible to do (Holton 2008, 51–55; Marsili 2016, 303–7). This means that intentions can't roam free: by uttering 'I'm waiting for you at the bar' I cannot intend to express the proposition *that the square root of four is two.*

Since victims of Moses illusions (and many other misspeakers alike) are trying to communicate what they believe to be true (and are under the mistaken impression that they can do it with the words they picked), INTENTIONAL EXPRESSION handles these utterances correctly. Interestingly, even though it doesn't mention higher-order beliefs, this view also gives the correct verdict for cases of fragmented belief like (4). A speaker who intends to express a proposition they believe to be true will assert their conscious, higher-order, belief, even if this doesn't correspond to their subconscious, or lower-order, attitudes. Consequently, as things stand, INTENTIONAL EXPRESSION fares better than all of its rivals.[18]

2.3 The Manipulation View: Hearer-Centred Sincerity

According to its detractors, the expression view overlooks the importance of the receiving end of the communicative exchange: the audience (aka the hearer, or the recipient). When people communicate, it's often to get other people to think something or to do something. Perhaps, then, the essence of communication (its primary function, what makes it important and useful) rather resides in its ability to influence other people's thoughts and actions. I shall call this the *contagion* or *manipulation* model, because it focuses on how mental states can hop from one mind to another (hence contagion), and how communicators can influence their recipient's thoughts and action, often to their advantage (hence manipulation). If the expression view is *speaker-centred* (it takes communication to be about expressing the internal states of *the speaker*), the contagion view is *hearer-centred* (it's about how communication affects *the hearer*).

---

work (Marsili 2017, 29–30; 2018a, n. 8; 2021a, 504; 2021b, 3258) I defended a version of the intentional expression view. Pepp (2018) expresses sympathy for intentionalism, but finds it wanting. Stokke (2018, 192) offers a more sophisticated version of this view; on top of an important trade-off in complexity, I worry that his proposal leads to some imprecise predictions – see footnote 39.

[18] This account (given the caveat introduced in footnote 15) also seems able to handle some puzzles described in Pepp 2018 (cf. Marsili 2021a).

In animal communication studies, communication is almost invariably conceived of as a form of manipulation – as a system of 'signal–response' pairs. Take the bright colouration of noxious frogs, which signals toxicity. Its function is to trigger a certain behaviour in the receiver – specifically, to get predators not to eat the frog. Receivers evolved to comply because they have something to gain from executing the appropriate response – they avoid poisoning or death. Generalising, the function of animal signals is typically to manipulate the receiver's behaviour.[19]

Ruth Millikan famously extended this model to human communication. In Millikan's framework, the evolutionary function of assertion (the purpose for which it was selected and passed on from generation to generation – its 'proper function') is to *persuade* the audience that its content is true (2005, ch. 8) – in other words, to manipulate the thoughts of the audience.

Another influential defender of the manipulation model is H.P. Grice. For Grice (1989) and his followers, genuine communication ('non-natural meaning') arises when agents produce utterances that are intended to alter the mental states of their receivers in certain ways. Specifically, to mean that p is to have a reflexive intention (R-intention) to get the hearer to believe p (at least partly) because of their recognition that we intend them to believe that p. Here, too, communication is understood as an attempt to influence the mental states of the receiver.

Under this family of views, sincere and insincere speech can be distinguished by their differential intended effects on the audience. Sincere speech is about *coordination* or *contagion*: the beliefs of speaker and hearer are meant to match. Insincere speech, by contrast, is about *manipulating* thought (hence mismatch is the goal) – see Figure 2.

There are different ways to articulate this idea into a definition; much depends on which precise intention is deemed essential. For instance, the early Grice (1957) understands communication as an attempt to get the audience to believe *that what the speaker said is true*. Some subsequent formulations, by both Grice and his followers, rather understood communication as an attempt to get the audience to believe *that the speaker believes that what they said is true*. More complex formulations have been proposed[20]; limiting our attention to the first two models, we get the following account of sincerity (with its 'higher-order' variation in square brackets):

---

[19] Many complications emerge, especially in modelling deceptive signals (such as those sent by non-noxious frogs with bright colouration). For an introduction, see Smith and Harper 2003, Searcy and Nowicki 2005, and Graham 2020.

[20] Alternatives include Grice 1989 (ch. 5), Strawson 1964, Schiffer 1972, and Bach and Harnish 1979.

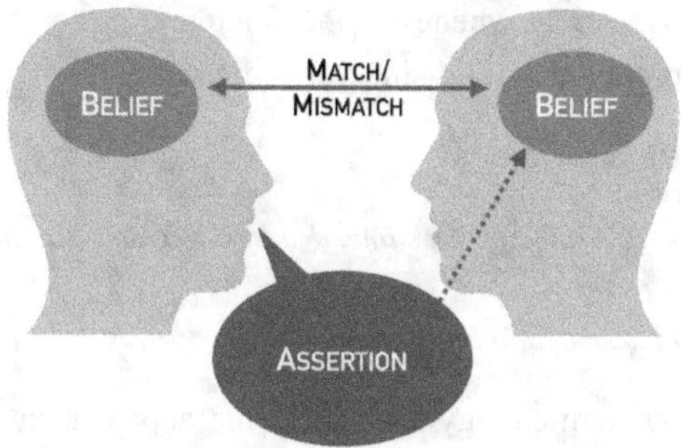

Figure 2 A representation of hearer-centred views, highlighting its focus on the intended outcome: sincerity depends on whether the assertion is expected to cause the hearer's belief to match the speaker's.

STANDARD HEARER-CENTRED
Sincerity depends on whether the speaker S intends their assertion to cause their audience A's belief to match theirs.

* *An assertion with content p is sincere iff S intends that assertion to cause A to believe [that S believes] p, and S believes p to be true.*

* *An assertion with content p is insincere iff S intends that assertion to cause A to believe [that S believes] p, and S believes p to be false.*

This conception retains important similarities with speaker-centred views: ultimately, whether the speaker believes the relevant proposition determines its sincerity. A speaker who satisfies STANDARD HEARER-CENTRED conditions for sincerity (or insincerity) thereby satisfies STANDARD EXPRESSION conditions, although the opposite isn't true: satisfying speaker-centred conditions doesn't entail satisfying hearer-centred conditions. This view is thus *stronger* than its speaker-centred counterpart – it imposes higher standards for both sincerity and insincerity. Only statements that are intended to cause a certain doxastic[21] effect on the audience can be deemed sincere or insincere. Contagion theorists will see no problem here: in their view, genuine (assertoric) communication requires an intention to persuade (though we'll see some arguments against this idea in the next section).

Intermediate positions are possible. For Williams (2002), only *insincerity* requires an intention to affect the beliefs of the audience: 'Sincere assertions do not necessarily have the aim of informing the hearer; but insincere assertions do have the aim of misinforming the hearer' (Williams 2002, ch. 4.2). The result is

---

[21] *Doxastic* is a technical term, meaning 'pertaining to belief'.

that one asserts insincerely whenever one is attempting to get the audience to believe a[22] false proposition, and sincerely otherwise.

DECEPTIVE HEARER-CENTRED

- *An assertion is insincere iff it's intended by S to cause A to believe a false proposition.*
- *An assertion is sincere otherwise.*

Introducing some terminology is helpful for appreciating some systematic differences between the definitions. STANDARD HEARER-CENTRED is a 'bound' conception of sincerity, because it ties sincerity to a particular proposition: whether the speaker is sincere depends on whether the speaker is attempting to get the audience to believe *a particular proposition.* By contrast, DECEPTIVE HEARER-CENTRED is 'unbound': it doesn't specify which false proposition one has to aim to instil in the audience. Additionally, since sincerity is defined as the absence of insincerity, I'll say that DECEPTIVE HEARER-CENTRED is a 'mirrored' definition.

Of course, more definitions can be developed by combining the elements reviewed so far. We can make STANDARD HEARER-CENTRED into a mirrored definition by defining sincerity as the absence of insincerity, or into an unbound definition by removing its ties to a specific proposition. The exact intention required, the target proposition, etc. can also be changed.[23] There are so many options that attempting to list them all would be hopeless; for present purposes, what matters is that these definitions admit systematic variations.

Compared to speaker-centred conceptions of sincerity, which are orthodox in pragmatics and philosophy of language, hearer-centred conceptions are somewhat fringe views. Still, they have a long history. Aquinas already distinguished three ways in which assertions can fail to be true:[24]

> *[There can be falsehood] materially, since what is said is false, formally, on account of the will to tell an untruth, and effectively, on account of the will to impart a falsehood. (ST, II, 110,1)*

The *Doctor Angelicus* here differentiates between three notions. The first, 'material falsehood', indicates *falsity* (see Section 2.1.4) rather than *insincerity.* The second, 'formal falsehood', comes close to the 'intentional expression view' discussed in Section 2.2.2. Finally, 'effective falsehood'

---

[22] Williams rejects the idea that insincerity should be tied to a specific proposition: attempting to deceive about *any* proposition is enough to be insincere.

[23] See Eriksson 2011 (230) for a complex variation of STANDARD HEARER-CENTRED.

[24] Latin lacks a dedicated word for sincerity, so Aquinas's discussion of veracity (*veracitas*) covers sincerity and veracity at once.

is a hearer-centred conception of insincerity: the will to impart a falsehood comes very close to DECEPTIVE HEARER-CENTRED.[25]

Critics may argue that hearer-centred views conflate the notion of an *insincere* assertion with the notion of an assertion that is *intended to deceive*. DECEPTIVE HEARER-CENTRED certainly invites this equivalence.[26] To intend to deceive is to intend to instil a false belief, which is precisely how this view defines insincerity. If hearer-centred views conflate two notions that speaker-centred views hold separate, adopting them might impoverish our conceptual repertoire. While these considerations suggest that (in)sincerity is best defined in speaker-centred terms, there are also arguments in favour of hearer-centred conceptions of (in)sincerity. We do expect honest speakers to refrain from deceiving, and this expectation can reasonably be regarded as related to sincerity. To adjudicate whether hearer-centred conceptions really track something essential about sincerity, let's bring more considerations to the table, and move on to assess their ability to handle specific cases.

2.3.1 Bluffs

> *I never could tell a lie that anyone would doubt, nor a truth that anybody would believe.*
>
> Mark Twain, Following the Equator

Speaker-centred and hearer-centred views have important similarities, and their verdicts converge in most circumstances. But there is space for divergence, such as in the following example, which goes back to St. Augustine (here reinterpreted):

> TWO ROADS
> *Simplicius needs to choose between two paths to reach his destination. Marcellus, his business rival, knows that one road is teeming with bandits, while the other one is safe. He also knows that Simplicius will believe the exact opposite of whatever he claims. If Marcellus claims that the road on the right is safe, Simplicius will take the one on the left, and vice versa.*

What should Marcellus do? One option is to bluff: Marcellus can claim that the road with the bandits is safe, knowing that Simplicius will believe the opposite, and take the safe road. To simplify the discussion, let's call this option the

---

[25] Hearer-centred views are also discussed in Trilling 2009 (58), who argues that this distinction is paralleled by the French and English norms of sincerity: simply put, the French demand speaker-centred sincerity, whereas the English demand hearer-centred sincerity. While the suggestion is fascinating, the fact that most English philosophers and linguists defend speaker-centred conceptions of sincerity should give us pause.

[26] Although STANDARD HEARER-CENTRED does not treat them as fully equivalent, it still allows for a significant overlap between the two notions.

ALTRUISTIC UNTRUTH. Here Marcellus will get Simplicius's beliefs to match his, at the price of saying what he believes to be false. If Marcellus instead states what he believes to be true (namely, that the safe road is the safe one), his interlocutor's beliefs won't match his: Simplicius will end up believing the opposite, and will be robbed by bandits. I'll call this option the SELFISH TRUTH, on the assumption that Simplicius has some interest in getting his competitor out of business.

For speaker-centred views of all flavours, the ALTRUISTIC UNTRUTH is insincere (since it involves speaking *contra mentem*) and the SELFISH TRUTH sincere. STANDARD HEARER-CENTRED yields the opposite verdict: the ALTRUISTIC UNTRUTH is sincere (since it aims to achieve a doxastic match between hearer and speaker), whereas the SELFISH TRUTH is insincere (since it aims to achieve a mismatch).[27] DECEPTIVE HEARER-CENTRED, on the other hand, deems both utterances insincere: in both cases, Marcellus intentionally gets Simplicius to believe a false proposition: with the SELFISH TRUTH, that Marcellus does not believe what he said, and that what he said is not true;[28] with the ALTRUISTIC UNTRUTH, that Marcellus wanted him to believe what he said.

Which characterisation is correct? The ALTRUISTIC UNTRUTH ensures that Simplicius acquires a true belief: accusations of insincerity might be unfair here. However, in this case Marcellus also expresses a belief that he rejects (that the road is safe): it would seem too generous to deem his statement sincere. Augustine (who was rather concerned with whether the speaker would be *lying*) did not find a definitive solution. Personally, I have the intuition that Marcellus's ALTRUISTIC UNTRUTH would be *insincere* after all, and the SELFISH TRUTH *sincere*. Most authors agree (e.g. Moran 2005, 17; Mahon 2015, §1.2; Fallis 2010, 11), but there are exceptions (Chisholm and Feehan 1977, 153–54; Faulkner 2013). A more decisive case against hearer-centred views emerges from blatant lies.

2.3.2 Blatant Lies

E sappi, che tu troverai di molti che mentono, a niun cattivo fine tirando, né di proprio loro utile, né di danno o di vergogna altrui, ma perciocché la bugia per sé piace loro; come chi bee non per sete, ma per gola del vino.

Giovanni della Casa, *Galateo, overo De' Costumi*, XXIII

A blatant (or 'bald-faced') lie is a lie that cannot be meant to deceive, because there is mutual awareness that the speaker is lying, so that the speaker cannot believe that the audience can be persuaded. Here's an example:

---

[27] Not so for the 'higher order' version of STANDARD HEARER-CENTRED, whose predictions align with speaker-centred views here (if the qualification mentioned in the next footnote holds).

[28] Assuming that this is Marcellus's intention.

CCTV Camera[29]

Pete took part in a robbery. He knows that his involvement in the crime was unmistakably recorded on CCTV camera, so there is no chance that anybody will believe him if he denies that he was there. However, he also knows that if he denies being involved in the robbery, the judge will delay the trial and set a low bail. So he claims that he wasn't present at the scene of the crime. He has no intention to deceive anyone. He only says this because he is planning to skip bail.

Intuitively, Pete is lying, even if he lacks an intention to deceive his audience. Pete's goal in making a false assertion isn't to persuade the judge, but rather to motivate his audience to act in certain ways. This is but one example of a lie that is not meant to deceive. Countless more have been discussed in the literature – if you don't find CCTV Camera convincing, there's a strong chance that you will find that some other example better demonstrates the point.[30] This growing list of counterexamples has led most scholars to conclude that lying only typically, rather than necessarily, involves attempted deception.[31]

Related observations have been brought up against contagion views in general. Gricean accounts have taken quite a beating in the literature, and have somewhat fallen out of fashion in speech act theory, primarily due to their inability to account for 'non-manipulative' assertives – that is, claims that are not aimed at persuading their audience (see e.g. Aldrich 1966; Alston 2000, 44–50; Siebel 2003; 2020; García-Carpintero 2004; Green 2007, 75–82). Amendments have been proposed,[32] but these patches only manage to cover a portion of the objections raised. Wayne Davis (1999, 21–22) offers a pretty damning overview of the counterexamples faced by contagion views:

For example, if [the speaker] were proclaiming his innocence in the face of a mountain of incriminating evidence, affirming his beliefs before inquisitors forcing him to recant, talking to someone he knew did not trust him, uttering a platitude, answering a rhetorical question, reminding someone of an appointment, or answering a teacher. . . . Alternatively, the audience may be unperceptive, unintelligent, unconscious, or even dead, as when people speak to babies, pets, and the recently departed. More radically, there may not even be an intended audience, as when one is recording something in a private diary,

---

[29] This example, taken from Marsili 2023, is inspired by the 'Witness on CCTV' example (Carson 2006, 289–90) and the 'Cheating Student' example (290).

[30] Among them lies under coercion (Siegler 1966, 129), 'bald-faced lies' (Carson et al. 1982; Sorensen 2007), 'knowledge lies' (Sorensen 2010), 'tell-tale sign lies' (Krstić 2019), 'alternative motivation' lies (Rutschmann and Wiegmann 2017; Sneddon 2021), and many others (Marsili 2016, §9.2; 2021a, §2.3; Sorensen 2018).

[31] Some have resisted this conclusion, typically criticising the validity of certain examples. For an overview, see Mahon 2015 and Krstić 2023.

[32] For discussion, see again Grice 1989 (ch. 5), Strawson 1964, Schiffer 1972, and Bach and Harnish 1979.

> *scribbling notes to solve a problem, or venting frustrations by cursing loudly precisely because no one can hear.*

These are assertions that can clearly be sincere or insincere depending on context. However, for STANDARD HEARER-CENTRED they can be neither (since they cannot be intended to persuade the audience), and for DECEPTIVE HEARER-CENTRED they cannot be insincere (since they cannot be intended to persuade the audience of something false).

Recapitulating, contagion views face two related problems. On the sincerity side, speakers who assert don't always aim to persuade their audiences: STANDARD HEARER-CENTRED incorrectly predicts that these speakers are not being sincere. On the insincerity side, liars don't always intend to deceive, but hearer-centred views predict that their non-deceptive lies are not insincere. Crucially, no view that avoids both objections would be truly hearer-centred – since it would not require that the hearer's mental states be affected by the assertion.

This is not to say that contagion views are completely unhelpful for theorising about insincerity. Arguably, contagion views correctly identify the *prototypical* (cf. Rosch 1973) features of sincerity and insincerity. Even if assertoric communication does not *exclusively* aim at persuasion, this is its *primary* or *typical* goal. Liars paradigmatically aim to deceive, and sincere speakers to inform their interlocutors. There's a corollary to this: where the predictions of speaker-centred and hearer-centred views diverge, we have non-paradigmatic cases of sincerity and insincerity. A sincere speaker who doesn't aim to persuade their audience is still making a sincere assertion, but their intentions are somewhat atypical; the same goes for the liar who lacks an intention to deceive.

Relatedly, a liar who intends to deceive arguably is *more insincere* than a liar who hopes they won't be believed, or who is indifferent about the outcome of their utterance. If this is right, hearer-centred views capture something about insincerity that speaker-centred views fail to grasp. Even though deceptive intent isn't necessary for insincerity, deceptive intentions affect the *degree* or *extent* to which a statement is insincere.[33] Far from simply being on the wrong track, then, hearer-centred conceptions complement our understanding of what sincerity is. Appropriately incorporated (as an account of paradigmatic cases), they help us quantify how insincere a speaker can be, introducing more nuance to the picture delineated by the expression view.

Both speaker-centred and hearer-centred views admit further refinement, to accommodate phenomena like non-literal meaning, non-assertoric speech, and uncertainty. The following sections deal with these complications.

---

[33] I doubt that the same can be said of sincere speech: intending to persuade the audience does not make your sincere assertion more sincere.

2.4 Literally Sincere, Indirectly Deceptive

In the landmark case for perjury statute, *Bronston v. United States* (409 US 352, 1973), the defendant (Bronston) was asked if he ever owned a Swiss bank account. He responded:

(5)   The company had an account there for about six months, in Zurich.

In fact, Bronston himself had owned a bank account in Switzerland. Although (5) is literally truthful, it's also meant to convey something false, namely that Bronston (rather than the company) never had a Swiss account. The US Supreme Court eventually ruled that Bronston's statement, being literally true, did not amount to perjury. However, it would be a stretch to say that Bronston answered the question sincerely. If this intuition is on the right track, insincere speech extends beyond literal communication.

In the specialised literature, non-literal statements that indirectly convey a believed-false proposition are said to be misleading, but not lies (Saul 2012).[34] The distinction between lying and 'merely misleading', in turn, is typically understood to be grounded in the distinction between *what is said* and *what is implicated*[35] (or the related distinctions between *literal* and *non-literal* content, *explicit* vs *implicit*, *asserted* vs *implied*, etc.). Besides its theoretical interest, the distinction has practical implications: it's clearly important for legislative purposes (Green 2018), and is said to have moral (Adler 1997; Strudler 2009) and epistemic (Fricker 2012) implications.

An advantage of choosing indirect deception (misleading) over lying is that it strategically preserves deniability. A speaker who *merely implies* (without explicitly asserting) a deceptive message is able to deny, without contradiction, that they meant to convey the deceptive content. If accused by the prosecution of having claimed that he never *personally* owned a Swiss account, Bronston could have insisted, 'That's not what I meant, you misunderstood me: I only said that the company had an account there'. Deniability is sought by deceivers because it makes it more difficult to hold them accountable for what they communicated (Pinker et al. 2008; Saul 2024).

As anticipated earlier, accounts of sincerity can be distinguished based on whether they are 'bound' and 'unbound'. *Bound* views tie sincerity to the explicit, semantic content of the relevant assertion. On these views, merely misleading utterances like (5) count as sincere. Since Bronston believes the

---

[34] This distinction is standard, but not without its detractors. Some reject it altogether (Meibauer 2005; 2014), others argue that it does not fully overlap with the distinction between saying and implicating (Viebahn 2017; 2021; but cf. Marsili and Löhr 2022).

[35] The noun 'implicature' and the adjective 'implicated' are technical terms introduced by Grice (1989). For a primer, see Davis 2010.

literal content of his assertion, he is sincere by *bound* speaker-centred standards. *Unbound* views, by contrast, don't tie sincerity to any specific propositional content, meaning that indirect communication can be classified as insincere.

Should sincerity be modelled along bound or unbound lines? Calling misleading statements like (5) 'sincere' may sound hopelessly lenient. Academics haven't much considered the issue, and only a few scholars explicitly acknowledge that misleading statements fall under the remit of insincere speech (Eriksson 2011, 230; Stokke 2018, 190–93). Luckily, any bound view can be converted into its unbound counterpart, with some simple adjustments. If a view of sincerity requires that the literal content p meet condition C, its bound version can be derived by requiring instead that *all the propositions the speaker intentionally communicates* (*both* the literal *and* the non-literal ones) meet condition C (otherwise the assertion is insincere). Applied to the STANDARD EXPRESSION, for example, we obtain the following unbound (mirrored) view:

UNBOUND STANDARD EXPRESSION
Given a speaker S who, in making an assertion, expresses[36] *a set of propositions P:*

- *The assertion is sincere iff S believes all members of P.*
- *The assertion is insincere otherwise.*

This gets the desired results. Misleading statements like (5), as well as canonical lies, are classified as insincere, since both communicate believed-false propositions. To be sincere, the speaker must believe both the literal and non-literal contents. The same formula can be applied to convert any bound account of insincerity into an unbound one.[37]

Bound sincerity is always 'stricter' than its unbound counterpart, since all the communicated propositions (and not just the literal content of the statement) must meet the sincerity condition (whatever we take it to be). An advantage of unbound views is that they seem to better track ordinary language use: intuitively, Bronston's statement isn't fully sincere. Additionally, these views display sensitivity to another way in which insincerity can be incremental. Arguably, the more believed-false propositions the speaker communicates, the more insincere their statement is. Just as the presence (or absence) of a deceptive intent can increase (or decrease) how insincere a statement is, so too can the communication of multiple contents affect the strength of our ascriptions of insincerity.

---

[36] Of course, what the speaker 'expresses' here covers both what's communicated explicitly and what's communicated implicitly or indirectly.

[37] Similarly, by the same token, any unbound view can be converted into a bound one, by tying sincerity *only* to the literal content of the utterance.

2.5 That's Bullshit!

In 1986, Harry Frankfurt published an influential article that identified a form of insincere discourse that didn't fit the standard categories: *bullshit*. While lying requires saying what you believe to be false, bullshitting is a matter of asserting propositions whose veracity you have not even assessed. The goal of the bullshitter is often not persuasion, but something altogether different, such as impressing or appeasing their audience. Here's an example:

> PRESIDENTIAL BULLSHIT
> *Pressed by journalists while leaving a government building, the president doesn't fully grasp the question she was asked. She has no idea of what the journalists are talking about, but she wants to give the impression that she has everything under control. She replies:*
>
> (6) *The party is taking serious measures to resolve the problems you just mentioned. We have our best people working on this issue!*

Here the president responds with (6) to project an image of confidence to the press. She has no idea whether the party is taking measures to resolve the problems mentioned by the journalists. As Frankfurt (1986, 125) would put it,

> *[Her] statement is grounded neither in a belief that it is true nor, as a lie must be, in a belief that it is not true. It is just this lack of connection to a concern with truth – this indifference to how things really are – that I regard as of the essence of bullshit.*

Frankfurt rightly notes that, far from being a fringe phenomenon, bullshit is widespread, notably in political speech and advertisement. The typical example of a bullshitter is the car salesman, or the politician who 'never yet considered whether any proposition were true or false, but whether it were convenient for the present minute or company to affirm or deny it' (Swift 1710).[38]

So far, I implicitly assumed that either a speaker believes a proposition to be true, or they believe it to be false. Call this useful simplification the *dichotomous model* of belief, since it assumes that there are only two doxastic states: belief in the truth of a proposition, and belief in its falsity.

Bullshit throws a third state into the mix: the state of being agnostic (lacking a belief), which is characteristic of this form of speech. It invites us to consider a *trichotomous model* of belief with three possible states: (i) believing p to be true,

---

[38] Sceptic philosophers, who engage in willing suspension of belief (*epoché*), famously do not have beliefs (or claim not to) on a wide variety of topics. It's unclear whether they are lying when they claim that they have no opinion about such mundane matters or whether they are bullshitting when (inconsistently with their doctrine) they make assertions about mundane matters they are supposed to lack opinions about.

(ii) believing *p* to be false, and (iii) lacking a belief about *p*. These three states broadly correspond to (i) standard sincerity, (ii) standard insincerity, and (iii) bullshit.

A good theory of sincerity should presumably acknowledge that bullshitting is a form of insincerity.[39] Intuitively, the BULLSHITTING PRESIDENT is insincere in claiming that the party is addressing the problem. However, traditional views (at least in their standard, bound formulations) deem bullshit neither sincere nor insincere. This is because bullshitters neither *believe* nor *disbelieve* the asserted proposition.[40]

Addressing this limitation requires integrating a trichotomous view of belief into standard accounts. This is as simple as revising the scope of the negation in any given account of insincerity – switching any requirement that 'S believes *not-p*' into the requirement that 'S does not believe that *p*'. To illustrate, here's two 'wide scope' versions of classic accounts of insincerity:

> INTENTIONAL EXPRESSION (WIDE-SCOPE INSINCERITY)
> *An assertion is insincere iff in making it, the speaker intends to express a proposition that S does not believe to be true.*
>
> STANDARD HEARER-CENTRED (wide-scope insincerity)
> *An assertion with content p is insincere iff it's intended by S to cause A to believe [that S believes] p, and S doesn't believe p to be true.*

These wide-scope definitions of insincerity correctly acknowledge that bullshit is insincere.[41] Since the president lacks an opinion about her assertion,

---

[39] Even broader definitions of bullshit are available, but presumably they go beyond *insincere* bullshitting, which is my focus here. Carson (2010, 62) and Stokke (2018, 140–59) argue that *evading questions* and *filibustering* with believed-true statements amounts to bullshitting. Insofar as these statements (and their implicatures) are believed to be true, they are sincere (regardless of whether they are bullshit), and so irrelevant for my purposes. (Incidentally, however, if this observation is correct, it undermines Stokke's definition of insincerity; cf. Stokke 2018, 192). Cohen (2002) famously suggests that bullshit can also be a matter of content. *Unclarifiable unclarity* or *pseudo-profound bullshit* like 'hidden meaning transforms unparalleled abstract beauty' (Pennycook et al. 2015) is bullshit regardless of the speaker's attitude towards them. I agree, but I would insist that such bullshit is insincere only when the speaker lacks a belief in its content: if they genuinely believe their own bullshit, I see no problem in saying that they are sincerely asserting pseudo-profound bullshit.

[40] By contrast, unbound views like DECEPTIVE HEARER-CENTRED classify bullshit as insincere because of its misleadingness. As Frankfurt (1986, 130) notes, the bullshitter 'necessarily attempt[s] to deceive us about … his enterprise' (i.e. about whether they have evaluated the veracity of their assertion).

[41] Frankfurt may disagree that hearer-centred views capture all cases of bullshit, since he holds that 'the bullshitter may not deceive us, or even intend to do so, either about the facts or about what he takes the facts to be' (1986, 54). However, Frankfurt also requires that bullshitters must aim to deceive their audience about their enterprise. Consequently, 'indifferent' bullshit would still be captured by at least *some* HEARER-CENTRED conceptions (such as DECEPTIVE HEARER-CENTRED).

she doesn't believe that its content is true: both views therefore classify (6) as insincere.

2.6 Degrees of Sincerity

The opposite of truth has many shapes, and an indefinite field

Montaigne, *Essays, 1, IX (On Lying)*

The trichotomous conception of doxastic states is better suited to modelling sincerity, especially in relation to bullshit. While this is surely an improvement over the dichotomous paradigm, it still relies on a heavily simplified picture. Belief is still modelled as a psychological state that doesn't admit of degrees. *If* you believe something, you either believe that its content is true, or that it's false – no intermediate states are allowed. Arguably, however, beliefs (and sincerity) admit various intermediate degrees; if this is right, the trichotomous model still lacks nuance.

We will now explore two ways in which sincerity comes in degrees, in ways that aren't quantifiable by trichotomous accounts. First, there are *degrees of precision*, as in assertions that are believed to be *only partially true*. Second, there are *degrees of confidence*, as in assertions that are *only partially believed* to be true.[42]

2.6.1 Degrees of Precision

You believe that our common friend Vladimir, who stands at 190 cm high, is tall. But you have recently bought a shrinking ray. Let's remove a few centimetres from Vladimir's height, then. Now Vlad is 180 cm. Now he's 170. Now 160. As the literature on soritical progressions (e.g. Sorensen 2023) stresses *ad nauseam*, there presumably isn't a precise threshold at which our increasingly smaller friend stops being tall and starts being short (or not tall). Instead, as we proceed down the line (illustrated in Figure 3), describing Vladimir as 'tall' becomes progressively less accurate. Some would say that the proposition *that Vlad is tall* becomes 'less and less true'.

As we see Vladimir shrinking, our beliefs go through a series of intermediate states not fully captured by the trichotomous and dichotomous model. After Vlad's compression begins, at some point we will opine that the proposition *that Vladimir is tall* is only 'partially true', or not fully accurate, or imprecise; as the progression continues, we will eventually be inclined to think that it's false that he is tall. With some idealisation, we might say that there are infinitely many

---

[42] The sincerity of a statement is also affected by its *degree of strength*. I have no space to explore this here, but see Marsili 2014; 2018a for discussion.

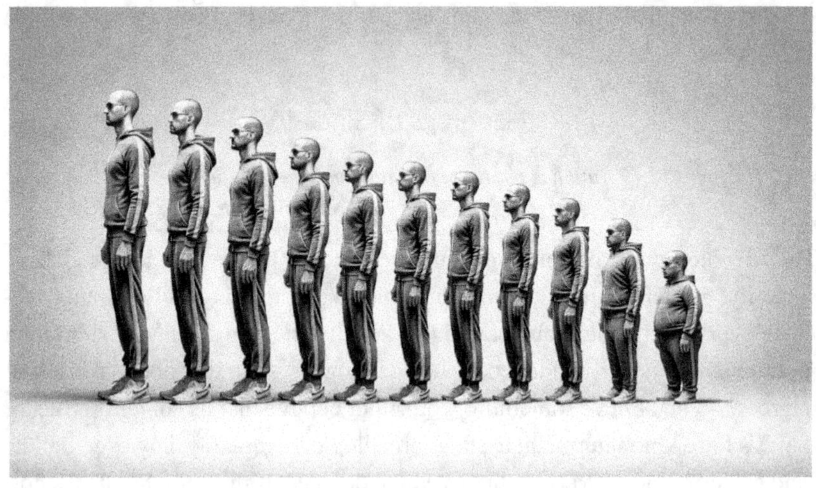

Figure 3 A scale of shrinking Vladimirs.

intermediate mental states between belief and disbelief, depending on 'how true' we take the proposition to be. Let's call these intermediate states *fuzzy beliefs*: they differ from unreserved full beliefs, because the observer only takes their content to be *partially accurate* (or inaccurate).

Fuzzy logic, which allows for graded truth-values, offers resources to formalise this idea. Numerical values going from 0 (false) to 1 (true) can be assigned to propositions to measure 'how true' they are. Let's then assign decreasing numerical truth-values to the proposition that Vladimir is tall, as we evaluate it at different times: the proposition that Vladimir is tall at time 1 (call it V_1) will have a truth-value of 1, the proposition V_2 (that Vladimir is tall at time 2) a truth-value of 0.9, V_3 a truth-value of 0.8, and so forth. These intermediate degrees of truth are modelled by relying on an infinitely divisible scale of decimal numbers.

Sincerity can accordingly be conceived as a graded property, which goes from full sincerity to full insincerity, through a series of intermediate cases. Affirming that 'Vladimir is tall' at different stages of the transition (i.e. V_1, V_2, V_3, etc.) would be progressively less sincere. The first assertion would be backed up by a belief that p is fully true (sincere assertion, truth value of V_1 = 1); as we'd progress, this would give way to a belief that p is partially true (partially sincere assertion, truth value of V_3 = 0.8), until we arrived at a belief that p is fully false (insincere assertion, truth value of V_n = 0). So understood, sincerity comes in degrees: some assertions are more sincere than others, some more insincere. If I tell you that Vladimir is tall at time 1, I am definitely being sincere; if I tell you the same at time n, I am definitely being insincere. But what should be said about the cases that fall around the midpoint?

With its numerical, quantifiable account of how 'true' assertions are, this model suggests an apparently appealing solution to this problem. There is an intermediate threshold between truth and falsity: 0.5. Assertions falling below this value are considered falser than they are true, and those falling above it are considered truer than they are false. A natural conclusion is that sincerity and insincerity, too, will follow a similar pattern.[43] Applying this insight to STANDARD EXPRESSION, we can derive the following criterion (cf. Marsili 2014, 157–8):

FUZZY
- *An assertion is sincere iff the speaker believes its content to be more than 0.5-true.*

- *An assertion is insincere otherwise.*

All idealisations, however, come at the price of some distortions. Two are worth noting here. First, as it's currently formulated, this view posits a sharp threshold: assertions with truth-values above 0.5 count as sincere, those below as insincere. But as truth-values increase, we should rather expect a progressive, gradual transition from insincerity to sincerity: like 'tall', 'sincere' presumably behaves like a graded predicate with fuzzy boundaries. Ideally, then, an account of sincerity should acknowledge that sincerity admits of degrees and lacks a sharp transition point (cf. Isenberg 1964, 470; Marsili 2014; 2018a; 2022).

Second, it's psychologically unrealistic to assume that speakers invariably compute and assign numerical truth-values to propositions – especially given that there are statements that won't easily admit such numerical quantification. While partial beliefs are widespread, numerically quantifiable ones are not. To see this, consider the proposition p, *that Ugo is being unfaithful to his wife*. This proposition might be 'partially true' in different ways:

(a) Ugo has let someone steal a drunken kiss from him;
(b) Ugo has a crush he will never act upon;
(c) Ugo is flirting on dating apps, but he's not planning to meet anyone;
(d) Ugo has slept with someone else once and deeply regrets it.

---

[43] What about statements that fall exactly in-between? I will soon argue that we should refrain from forcing intermediate cases under a specific category. According to this first pass at a definition, however, sincerity requires a truth-value *above* 0.5, meaning that a value of 0.5 would yield an insincere statement.

Under all these circumstances, *p* is at most *partially true*. But it's not clear that we can numerically quantify 'how true' *p* is under each circumstance. Surely we don't reason numerically when we consider whether asserting a proposition would be appropriate: there are qualitative considerations that don't easily translate into quantitative assessments. On the other hand, we seem to have opinions about how *close* to the truth these assertions are – that is, *p*'s differential proximity to truth in each circumstance. For example, one might feel that *p* is increasingly true as we move from (a) to (d) (or that some other order holds).

This suggests that sincerity has less to do with a precise numerical assessment than with some coarse-grained internal phenomenology – the speaker's perception of how true the assertion is. Supposing that sincerity depends on this 'perceived proximity to truth' (cf. Pepp 2024), and building upon STANDARD EXPRESSION for simplicity, we get:

PERCEIVED ALETHIC PROXIMITY
The sincerity of an assertion depends on how close to truth that assertion is perceived to be by the speaker S.

- *An assertion is sincere if S believes its content to be closer to truth than it is to falsity.*
- *An assertion is insincere if S believes its content to be closer to falsity than to truth.*

PERCEIVED ALETHIC PROXIMITY (perceived proximity to truth) is just as principled as FUZZY. Whenever the speaker numerically assesses the truth-value of the asserted proposition, these criteria output identical classifications: an assertion that is believed to have a truth-value superior (or inferior) to 0.5 is also an assertion that is perceived to be closer to (or further from) truth than falsity. However, PERCEIVED ALETHIC PROXIMITY (henceforth ALETHIC PROXIMITY, for short) has wider reach: it also covers circumstances where it's unrealistic to demand a numerical assessment of the proposition.

Additionally, ALETHIC PROXIMITY doesn't posit a sharp transition from sincerity to insincerity. Instead, sincerity is presented as a matter of degree: the closer to truth an assertion is believed to be, the greater its sincerity; the opposite applies to insincerity. This allows for intermediate cases: if a speaker finds it hard to establish whether an assertion is closer to truth or falsity, it's equally unclear whether that assertion is sincere or insincere. Rather than a sharp transition from sincerity to insincerity, we have a graded boundary and intermediate cases.

Finally, this revised criterion performs better in determining how insincere an assertion is. Consider the following scenario (from Pepp 2024):

EXAM UNDERSTATEMENT
Two students, Jane and Sue, have just received their scores on an important exam. Jane says to Sue, 'Oh Sue, I'm so upset – I only scored 55 on the exam! What did you get?' Sue looks down at her exam with a perfect score of 100 noted at the top. She knows from past experience that telling Jane the truth will only make her angry and resentful. She decides to lie about her score. Now consider two lies Sue might tell:

(7)   *I got 55.*

(8)   *I got 90.*

While (8) is comparatively closer to the truth, it's not 'partially true'. On the contrary, both (7) and (8) are plainly false: they both have a truth-value of 0. According to FUZZY, Sue is equally insincere in both cases. ALETHIC PROXIMITY offers a more nuanced verdict. Also by this criterion, both statements are insincere. However, (7) is correctly deemed *more insincere* by ALETHIC PROXIMITY, since sincerity 'depends on how close to truth that assertion is perceived to be by the speaker', and Sue perceives (8) to be closer to truth than (7).[44]

Crucially, graded insincerity isn't just a philosophical construction: it has important real-life implications. In *The Art of the Deal*, whose candid exposition of strategic dishonesty would prove prophetic, Trump writes:

The final key to the way I promote is bravado. I play to people's fantasies. People may not always think big themselves, but they can still get very excited by those who do. That's why a little hyperbole never hurts. People want to believe that something is the biggest and the greatest and the most spectacular. I call it truthful hyperbole. It's an innocent form of exaggeration – and a very effective form of promotion.

---

[44] Pepp (2024) proposes a similar solution. In her view, the sincerity of a statement (in reply to a question) depends both on ALETHIC PROXIMITY and 'subjective completeness' (how fully the reply, if true, would answer the question). This generates counterintuitive results: uninformative replies (e.g. (A): 'Either planets have circular orbits, or they don't', which has minimal subjective completeness and maximal alethic proximity) are deemed less sincere than distorting but informative approximations (e.g. (B): 'Planets describe circular orbits around the Sun'). Intuitively, however, tautologies like (A) can be fully sincere, unlike distortions like (B), which partially misrepresent the facts. This is not to deny that, under some conditions, uninformative replies like (A) can be insincere. This happens whenever an incomplete answer intentionally implies that the speaker lacks knowledge of the full answer (as predicted by unbound definitions). However, in contexts where no such 'ignorance implicature' arises (e.g. uttering (A) to *transparently* refuse to answer the question), Pepp's view predicts that uninformative replies are insincere *in virtue of being incomplete*, which seems to conflate insincerity with uncooperativeness.

We might disagree with Trump on whether purposeful exaggeration, especially in public discourse or business negotiations, is 'innocent' and 'never hurts'. But Trump's comments, if only accidentally, reveal something true – namely, that dishonest communicators like him can willingly exploit sincerity's gradation to mitigate the social consequences of deception. If I assert propositions that are totally false, the reputational risks are high. If I make assertions that are only partially insincere, the risks are smaller: charitable audiences might think that I just made a small mistake, or engaged in an 'innocent exaggeration'. This strategy is especially effective in political discourse, where partisan affiliation naturally favours charitable interpretations.[45] Studying degrees of insincerity, then, can help us better understand the grey area in which liars thrive.

2.6.2 Degrees of Confidence

Statements can be regarded as 'truer' or 'falser', generating intermediate doxastic states. Certainty and uncertainty, too, generate a doxastic continuum that isn't captured by the dichotomous or trichotomous model. Not all beliefs are equally strong: some we hold with more confidence (I'm certain that I'm in Madrid now), some with less (I'm somewhat confident that it's not yet 8 p.m.). By presenting ourselves as being more (or less) confident than we actually are, we can misrepresent our doxastic states. Does this constitute a form of insincerity? And if so, under which circumstances?

Like graded truth, graded confidence can be modelled by quantifying possible credal states on a numerical scale. Credences (i.e. doxastic states falling short of belief) can be assigned real numbers from 0 to 1, where 0 indicates certainty in the falsity of p, 1 indicates certainty in the truth of p, and 0.5 indicates absolute uncertainty – cases in which the subject regards p as equally likely to be true or false (see Figure 4).

So, for example, I'm absolutely certain *that I'm in Madrid right now* – I have a credence of 1. While I believe *that I will have a beer with my friends this*

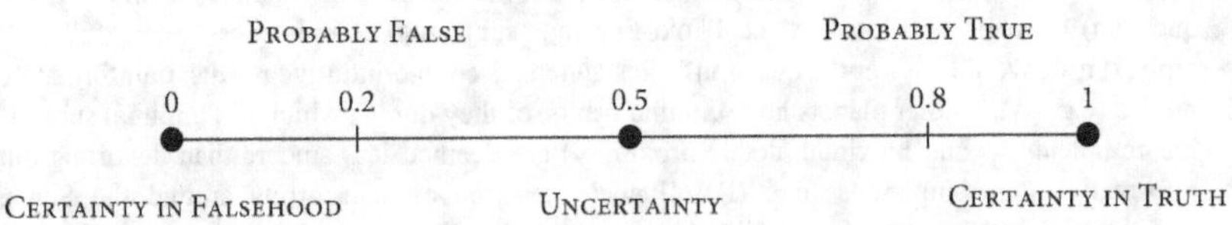

Figure 4 A visual representation of the certainty–uncertainty continuum.

---

[45] For an interesting take on the reputational dynamics of false statements directed at audiences split along partisan lines, see Saul 2024.

Saturday, I'm aware that the plan might be cancelled for whatever reason – I hold a credence of 0.8. Finally, while I think *that Barcelona will win the Clásico tonight*, I merely regard this as a likely possibility – a credence of 0.6.

Such graded beliefs pose challenges similar to those raised by graded truth-values. To illustrate, suppose that Trump, at the end of his term, exercises his bravado by claiming (9), in circumstances in which he regards this statement as *probably false*:

(9)   We enacted the biggest tax cuts in American history.[46]

Would (9) be sincere or insincere? More generally, where should we draw the boundary between sincere and insincere utterances when graded confidence is involved?

Once again, the temptation is to think that the threshold must fall precisely on the midpoint, at 0.5. While this idealisation yields the right result for Trump's (9) (classifying it as a lie), it falls into the same trap faced by FUZZY. Assuming that our credal states always admit numerical quantifications accessible to the speaker is psychologically unrealistic. When I consider whether Barcelona will win the Clásico, I might have a *feeling* of how confident I am in Barcelona's victory. Unless I am in the business of gambling, however, I won't have computed a numerical assessment of the likelihood that Barcelona will win. An account that rather relies on the phenomenology of our doxastic states (how confident we feel) would be preferable.

In previous work (Marsili 2014; 2018a; 2023a), I suggested that the sincerity of a statement depends on the speaker's perception of the likelihood of their statement. If the speaker consciously regards the asserted proposition to be more likely to be true than false, then their statement leans towards sincerity rather than insincerity; if they regard it to be more likely to be false than true, the opposite applies:

COMPARATIVE
The sincerity of an assertion depends on its perceived likelihood.

- *S's assertion is sincere to the extent that S takes themselves to be more confident in the truth of its content than in its falsity.*
- *S's assertion is insincere to the extent that S takes themselves to be more confident in the falsity of its content than in its truth.*

Trump's assertion that his tax cuts were the biggest in history (9) is insincere by this criterion (since, ex hypothesi, he regards it as more likely to be false than

---

[46]   Trump made this claim during his State of the Union address on 30 January 2018. Fact-checkers agree that it's false: his cuts at the time ranked between the fourth and eighth biggest in American history, depending on the calculation method.

true), even if Trump isn't fully confident in its falsity. Additionally, had Trump uttered the same statement while being *certain* of its falsity, his utterance would have been *more* insincere, since degrees of sincerity depend on the perceived likelihood of the statement. Sincere statements, too, admit similar rankings: a statement stemming from certitude will, ceteris paribus,[47] be more sincere than the same statement stemming from lower degrees of confidence.

However, COMPARATIVE doesn't handle EXAM UNDERSTATEMENT correctly. For COMPARATIVE, a wild departure from the truth like (7) (claiming you got 55 instead of 100) is just as insincere as a smaller departure like (8) (claiming 90 instead of 100). This is because Jane knows that she got 100, meaning that she takes herself to be equally (maximally) confident in the falsity of both propositions.

Luckily, while COMPARATIVE cannot do what ALETHIC PROXIMITY does (capturing proximity to the truth), the opposite is arguably true: degrees of confidence are captured by ALETHIC PROXIMITY. If I regard p to be more likely to be true than q, p is closer to the truth than q from my perspective. If 'proximity to truth' is interpreted in this way, ALETHIC PROXIMITY is able to track two dimensions along which sincerity can be graded: *precision* ('how true' a statement is perceived to be) and *confidence* ('how likely to be true' a statement is perceived to be).[48]

2.6.3 Degrees of Epistemic Damage

For sympathisers of hearer-centred conceptions of sincerity, the picture sketched so far is at best incomplete: it fails to consider how confidence and perceived alethic proximity influence the hearer's side of the picture. The notion of *expected epistemic damage* (Krauss 2017) provides an elegant remedy to this gap.

Credences can be more or less *accurate*, depending on whether they match the optimal degree of confidence that an agent should have. For example, if there's an 80 per cent chance that it will rain in Madrid today, a credence of 0.8 in this proposition will be maximally accurate. By trusting what people tell us (their testimony), our credences can shift. Depending on whether we are pushed

---

[47] This qualification is important for two reasons. First, context can affect the degree of confidence that is conveyed by a statement: depending on what's at stake (is it a matter of life and death, or an idle remark?), mutual expectations, and so forth, the very same statement may express a higher or lower degree of confidence in the same proposition (Marsili 2014, 168–70). Second, countervailing normative factors (like expectations of politeness) might alter our mutual expectations of sincerity – I come back on this in Section 3.2.

[48] For both views, absolute uncertainty and bullshit fall at the (fuzzy) border between sincerity and insincerity. This is an important limitation if one considers bullshit to be a paradigmatic form of insincerity.

closer or further from accuracy, our credences might become *more* or *less* accurate. When testimony makes our credences less accurate, we can say that it causes 'epistemic damage'. Epistemic damage is quantifiable: it's the difference between the accuracy of the recipient's credences before and after trusting a statement.

For example, suppose that John's credence in the proposition that it will rain in Madrid is 0.9, but that it goes down to 0.3 after watching the weather report. Ex hypothesi, John's credence was only a decimal point away from maximal accuracy ($|0.8–0.9|= 0.1$), but that distance has now gone up to 0.5 ($|0.8–0.3|= 0.5$). The epistemic damage caused by the weather report is therefore 0.4, reflecting a loss of 0.4 points ($0.1–0.5 = −0.4$); in other words, John's credence has been pushed 0.4 points away from maximal accuracy.

Krauss argues that a speaker lies iff they expect to cause epistemic damage greater than 0 with respect to the proposition they asserted, conditional on the audience trusting them with respect to *p*. Applied to sincerity:

> WORSE-OFF
> *The sincerity of an assertion depends on its expected epistemic damage.*
>
> - *An assertion is sincere iff its expected epistemic damage is 0;*
> - *An assertion is insincere otherwise.*

WORSE-OFF tracks the extent to which a speaker's deceptive intent can be graded, providing a nuanced alternative to hearer-centred views.[49] However, WORSE-OFF faces substantial difficulties. First, it assumes that speakers compute the epistemic damage of their assertions. While this is a useful idealisation, it once again fails the desideratum of psychological plausibility. Second, WORSE-OFF entails that an assertion cannot be insincere if it is addressed to an audience that is already maximally convinced of its content. This paves the way for counterexamples, such as the following (inspired by Benton 2018):

> COOKIES
> *Kermit tells the Cookie Monster (10), while being maximally certain that (10) is false, and while being aware that the Cookie Monster is already maximally convinced that (10) is false (Kermit knows that the Cookie Monster is certain that there are some cookies left).*

(10) There are no cookies in the jar.

While Kermit is clearly insincere, he isn't attempting to modify the Cookie Monster's confidence in (10). The expected epistemic damage is not greater

---

[49] Although Krauss conceived this criterion to track degrees of confidence rather than closeness to truth, there is at least the potential to extend the notion of epistemic damage to alethic proximity.

than 0: Worse-off therefore classifies (10) as sincere, which is incorrect. Generalising, counterexamples of this sort[50] suggest that there is more to insincerity than altering the accuracy of the audience's beliefs. Causally contributing to preserving an inaccurate belief (as in Cookies) can also constitute deception (Chisholm and Feehan 1977, 144) and therefore (by hearer-centred standards) insincerity.[51] Finally, Worse-off remains open to many of the objections raised in Section 2.3 against hearer-centred accounts.

That noted, the positive observations made for hearer-centred views apply here too. Ceteris paribus, an assertion is more insincere if both speaker-centred and hearer-centred conditions are satisfied, and more so if its expected epistemic damage is greater. Hence, like other hearer-centred views, Worse-off identifies an additional dimension along which insincerity can increase and decrease.

2.7 Sincerity beyond Assertion

2.7.1 Beyond Belief Expression

Analytic philosophy of language initially focused on descriptive uses of speech: assertions and their truth-conditions. Other uses (such as orders, greetings, or questions) were mostly ignored. Until some philosophers reacted: Austin (1975) famously denounced this narrow focus as a 'descriptive fallacy'. A new research programme, speech act theory, was born. Its main goal: to study how speech extends beyond *fact-stating* uses, and to understand how speech can perform actions (like asking, greeting, or firing someone) that go beyond describing the world.

So far, for simplicity's sake, I have knowingly committed the descriptive fallacy denounced by Austin: only the conditions under which *fact-stating speech* (specifically, assertoric speech) is sincere have been discussed. It's now time to drop this simplification, and extend what we learned so far to non-assertoric speech.

Philosophers often use the term 'direction of fit' to distinguish two possible relations between a representation (mental or linguistic) and its corresponding state of affairs. We talk of a *fact-stating*[52] direction of fit when the representation is meant to match the world, as with beliefs and assertions. If I believe or assert 'The window is open', my belief or assertion is correct or successful if it matches reality. Instead, when it is the world that should be rearranged to match

---

[50] See Benton 2018 and Marsili 2022 for further criticisms.

[51] Standard hearer-centred views also face this objection, but can be amended to require that the speaker intend to cause the hearer to believe *or continue to believe* the target proposition. Worse-off, by contrast, cannot easily be revised in this way.

[52] Here I'm using my own terminology (Marsili 2023b, 175–76), instead of Searle's (1979) classic, but lexically confusing, distinction between word-to-world/world-to-word directions of fit.

a representation, we have a *behaviour-directing* direction of fit. This is the case for orders and desires. If I sternly command 'Open the window!', my order (and desire) is satisfied only when facts are rearranged to match the representation (i.e. when you open the window).

While the *fact-stating* vs *behaviour-directing* dichotomy captures a crucial distinction, it doesn't come close to covering the full richness of our illocutionary repertoire (the range of things we can do with language). Fact-stating uses come in a variety of strengths and varieties. Some speech acts, such as guesses and conjectures, present facts less forcefully than assertions; others, like solemn oaths, with even more force. Meanwhile, within behaviour-directing speech, some speech acts define actions that *the speaker* has to perform ('commissives' like promises), while others define actions that *the hearer* should perform ('directives' like orders and requests). Additionally, some speech acts challenge the simplistic dichotomy between *fact-stating* and *behaviour-directing*: for example, official declarations (like 'I declare you husband and wife') are meant to achieve both goals at once. The list could go on; for our purposes, what matters is examining how a theory of sincerity can grapple with this complexity.

Let's consider how non-assertoric speech can be handled by two familiar conceptions of communication – the *expression view* and the *manipulation view*. For the expression theorist, speech acts differ primarily because they have the function of expressing different mental states: not just *beliefs*, but also intentions, desires, regrets, and so forth. Searle (1969, 65) articulates the idea as follows:

> *To assert, affirm, state (that p) counts as an expression of belief (that p). To request, ask, order, entreat, enjoin, pray, or command (that A be done) counts as an expression of a wish or desire (that A be done). To promise, vow, threaten or pledge (that A) counts as an expression of intention (to do A). To thank, welcome or congratulate counts as an expression of gratitude, pleasure (at H's arrival), or pleasure (at H's good fortune).*

If different speech acts express different mental states, then sincerity depends not just on beliefs, but on a variety of states. Specifically, a given illocutionary act will be sincere iff the speaker has the psychological attitude expressed by that act. Conversely, it is insincere when the speaker fails to be in that mental state:

ILLOCUTIONARY EXPRESSION
- *The performance of an illocutionary act F(p) is sincere iff, in uttering F(p), S expresses an attitude $\Psi(p)$, and $S\Psi(p)$.*[53]

---

[53] '$S\Psi(p)$' denotes the speaker (S) possessing the attitude Ψ (e.g. belief) with content *p*.

- *The performance of an illocutionary act F(p) is insincere iff, in uttering F(p), S expresses an attitude Ψ(p), and ~SΨ(p).*

This schema yields sincerity conditions for specific speech acts, once we plug in a characterisation of a specific speech act. Paired with the orthodox assumption that assertions express belief, for example, ILLOCUTIONARY EXPRESSION yields the 'wide scope' version of STANDARD EXPRESSION: an assertion is sincere when the speaker believes it, and insincere when the speaker doesn't believe it. Plug in the standard view that promises express intentions, and the result is that promises are sincere when the speaker intends to fulfil them, and insincere when they don't. And so forth for other speech acts.[54]

What about hearer-centred views? For STANDARD HEARER-CENTRED, the goal of assertion is to get the audience to match the speaker's attitude: to persuade them of a content *p*. But STANDARD HEARER-CENTRED also admits a 'higher order' variation, where the goal is to make the audience believe that the speaker has the relevant attitude (i.e. to make them believe that *the speaker believes p*). This higher-order variation is better suited to accommodating non-assertoric speech. Suppose I tell you (11):

(11) I promise that I will pick up your grandma at the airport.

In uttering (11), my hearer-directed goal is to get you to believe that I intend to pick up your grandma at the airport: I want you to believe that I have the attitude (intention) expressed by my promise. But I don't want you to endorse the same attitude yourself (i.e. I don't want you to match my mental state by forming an equivalent intention to pick up your grandma). The same logic applies to other speech acts, like thanking: if I express gratitude, it's not to get you to also feel grateful, but rather to get you to believe that I am grateful. Generalising:

ILLOCUTIONARY MANIPULATION
- *The performance of an illocutionary act F(p) is sincere iff, in uttering F(p), S is attempting to induce B(SΨ(p)) in A, and SΨ(p).*[55]

- *The performance of an illocutionary act F(p) is insincere iff, in uttering F(p), S is attempting to induce B(SΨ(p)) in A, and ~SΨ(p).*

---

[54] To turn ILLOCUTIONARY EXPRESSION into a view that is also sensitive to degrees of sincerity (Section 2.6), it can be modified so that S is insincere to the extent that S is closer to possessing the relevant attitude than they are to not possessing the attitude (and conversely for sincerity, see Marsili 2017, 148–51, 2023b). Applied to assertion, this yields verdicts comparable to ALETHIC PROXIMITY and COMPARATIVE. For an extension of this model to speech acts that express multiple psychological states at once, see Marsili 2016.

[55] B here stands for 'belief', and A stands for 'audience'. Attempting to induce B(SΨ(p)) in A, then, means attempting to get the audience to believe that the speaker has an attitude Ψ towards *p*.

Like their assertoric counterparts, Illocutionary Manipulation and Illocutionary expression often converge in their verdicts: for instance, promises will be insincere when the speaker lacks the relevant intention. However, Illocutionary Manipulation requires an additional intention to get the audience to believe that the speaker is in a certain mental state, similar to its assertoric counterpart (the higher-order version of Standard Hearer-Centred). This opens the way for objections and counterexamples that parallel the ones reviewed in Section 2.3, such as blatant lies.

Different speech acts have different 'felicity conditions'.[56] So far, we implicitly assumed that only the violation of a subset of felicity conditions (sincerity conditions) yields insincerity. Unbound views challenge this perspective. Some philosophers (Alston 2000, 67–68, 94) argue that, in performing a speech act F (*p*), a speaker indirectly communicates that they are complying with their felicity conditions for F(*p*). If this is right, whenever the speaker knowingly but covertly violates any felicity condition, they intentionally communicate something they believe to be false – yielding insincerity for unbound views. For example, by issuing the order 'I command you to drink that bottle of water!' the speaker might indirectly communicate that they meet the felicity conditions for issuing the order: that they have the authority to issue that order, that they wish for the order to be fulfilled, that there is a bottle of water, and so forth. If any such proposition is believed to be false, the utterance would be insincere by most unbound standards, even if this wouldn't violate the speech act's sincerity conditions. The net result is that any covert, intentional violation of a felicity condition counts as insincerity by unbound standards.

2.7.2 Keeping Your Word

Read my lips: no new taxes.

George H. W. Bush

During his 1988 presidential campaign, George H. W. Bush promised that 'no new taxes' would be implemented. Once in office, however, he faced economic pressures, and ultimately agreed to a budget deal that included tax increases. Bush broke his promise, disappointing many Republican voters.

Promise-breaking is often considered to stand on a par with insincere assertion: we call promise-breakers liars, and both are ways to misrepresent reality in speech. However, on every account reviewed so far (including their 'illocutionary' expansions), promise-breaking is *not* treated as a form of insincerity: insofar as the speaker intended to fulfil their promise at the time of making it,

---

[56] The conditions that speakers are supposed to meet as they perform a specific speech act (see Austin 1975).

the promise is sincere. Sincerity is fully determined at the moment in which the utterance is *produced*. When a speaker sends a message (e.g. 'No new taxes'), whether that message is sincere or insincere depends on the speaker's mental states. Whether speakers stick to their commitments is irrelevant for traditional views.

Is orthodoxy correct in maintaining that only speech production is relevant to sincerity? Or can one's actions turn a promise uttered in good faith into an insincere promise? Arguably, 'being true to one's word' is a requirement of sincerity – especially if we think of sincerity as a virtue, rather than a property of statements (cf. Section 3.2). The sincere person 'talks the talk and walks the walk', because 'actions speak louder than words'.

This philosophical problem was first discussed in medieval philosophy. Assessing whether lying is always a sin, Aquinas considers the idea that 'it is a lie not to fulfill what one has promised' (ST, Q110, article 3, obj. 5), only to conclude that 'a man does not lie, so long as he has a mind to do what he promises, because he does not speak contrary to what he has in mind' (Q110, article 3, reply to obj. 5). All the while, Aquinas acknowledges that if the promisor 'does not keep his promise, he seems to act without faith in changing his mind' (Q110, article 3, reply to obj. 5).

When it comes to promises that get broken for reasons that are outside the speaker's control, it's hard to disagree with Aquinas. Let's go back to (11), my promise to pick up your grandma at the airport. Imagine I am intent on doing this, but despite taking all precautions, my car is destroyed in an accident (for which I bear no responsibility) while I'm on my way to the airport. Surely I was sincere, even if I broke my promise. Here the distinction between *veracity* and *sincerity* (Section 2.1.4) finds an analogue in promises. Like assertions, promises can be objectively 'false' (insofar as they fail to translate into the promised act) without being insincere.

Now consider another scenario. I promise (11), but then I change my mind. I can't be bothered to pick up your grandma at the airport, I have better things to do – like going out for a walk and an ice cream. When I promised to pick up your grandma, I genuinely intended to do it, and to stick to my promise regardless of how attractive an ice-cream-fuelled walk in the park might sound. But it turns out that I'm fickle, and I changed my mind.

Here, breaking the promise was entirely dependent on my own decisions. On top of the objective discrepancy between language and reality that is characteristic of falsity, my utterance displays the discrepancy between language and mind that is characteristic of insincerity: I expressed an intention to pick your grandma up, but then I dropped that intention as soon as it suited me. Crucially, my change in intention constitutes a normative failure. A promisor doesn't just communicate that they have a certain intention at the moment of promising: they guarantee that their intention is unwavering; that they will stick to it regardless of any change in their subjective preferences.

A tempting conclusion is that promise-breaking only constitutes insincerity when it's deliberate. This criterion distinguishes promises that are broken in good faith (the car crash scenario) from promises that are broken in bad faith (the ice-cream scenario). However, it's unclear that we can draw a principled distinction in this way: many cases resist straightforward classification. Keeping a promise might impose conspicuous costs on the speaker: substantial effort (economic, physical), resisting social or political pressure (as for Bush's promise not to raise taxes), or genuine sacrifice (resisting violent coercion, pain, death threats). Failing to resist some of these pressures would still constitute *deliberate* promise-breaking, though not in bad faith. These observations only scratch the surface of the complexities we encounter in real life. Orthodoxy has the advantage of throwing such complications out of the picture: if sincere promising boils down to what the speaker intends to do at the time of the utterance, these complexities become irrelevant.

Expressions like 'He promised sincerely, even if he ended up breaking the promise' provide additional reasons to favour orthodoxy. These expressions are perfectly meaningful, even when the promise is broken deliberately. They illustrate that ordinary language naturally distinguishes between honesty in speech and honesty in action. Conflating both dimensions under the same label runs the risk of impoverishing our conceptual repertoire. A preferable alternative is to use two distinct terms for what appear to be two distinct kinds of violations.

Falkenberg (1988) moves in this direction: he distinguishes between insincerity and disloyalty. Disloyalty is 'the intrapersonal analogue to disobedience: like commands can be disobeyed by the [addressee], so promises, pledges, promissory oaths or contracts can be broken by the speaker' (85). Sincerity is a matter of speech production (honesty in speech); disloyalty, a matter of speech compliance (honesty in action). Adopting this distinction has the virtue of preserving the idea that there is a core 'discursive' conception of sincerity (cf. Section 2.1), all while acknowledging that there are other ways in which speakers can fail to communicate honestly.

2.8 Sincerity So Far

Let's take stock. This Element began by delimiting its scope: sincerity in *discourse*. This leaves aside omissions, deceptive actions, and objective false-hoods. Within the domain of communication, I identified two main families of views: speaker-centred and hearer-centred. Each is grounded in a different understanding of the primary function of communication: respectively, expression and contagion/manipulation.

I suggested that the *intentional expression view* offers the most promising solution to the main difficulties faced by speaker-centred views (belief fragmentation and misspeaking): according to this account, whether an assertion is sincere depends on whether the speaker intends to express a proposition that they believe or disbelieve. Hearer-centred views, on the other hand, face more structural limitations, particularly in accommodating cases where the speaker lacks any intention to persuade the audience. Even so, they highlight an important sense in which speech can be said to be sincere or insincere.

The rest of this section dealt with increasingly complex scenarios. As we reviewed them, we shed some of the simplifying assumptions from which we started. The dichotomous model of belief was replaced by a trichotomous model, and then by a graded one. Similarly, we expanded our scope from literal to non-literal communication, and from assertoric communication to the full range of speech acts. The naïve model from which we started was replaced by a much fuller picture, which better captures the true complexity of human communication, and the role that sincerity plays in it.

I have not attempted to provide a single, unified account that handles all complications and counterexamples at once. There's a reason for this. Incremental adjustments are often fruitful and effective, but not always. The expression view admits an *intentional* version, which in turn admits a *wide scope* version, which in turn admits an *unbound* version: here additional refinements sum up nicely, and they only require simple tweaks. By contrast, incremental expansions to accommodate non-assertoric speech (as in ILLOCUTIONARY EXPRESSION), degrees of insincerity (as in ALETHIC PROXIMITY), and indirect speech (as in the *unbound version* of any view) demand much more baroque revisions. While I occasionally hinted at how such incremental amendments could be achieved, I have not tried to provide an all-encompassing definition, for the resulting formulation would be cumbersome and overly complex. Simplicity is also an important virtue, and whether a characterisation is satisfactory will depend in large part on what one wants to do with it: different conceptions of sincerity are appropriate for different explanatory purposes.

With this in mind, I have favoured a pluralistic stance. Simple accounts, improved by small incremental amendments, will suffice in most contexts. More complex formulations can be summoned when more precision or nuance is needed. For example, when the focus is on assertoric speech, operating with a definition that is sensitive to non-assertoric speech is unnecessary. But when a broader focus is appropriate, conceptions of sincerity apt to capture the phenomenon are available.

Accordingly, rather than a single correct definition, I offered the reader a versatile toolkit, which can be contextually applied, with different degrees of precision, to explore the various ways in which speech can be (or fail to be) sincere.

These tools will prove useful in the next section. While the first part of this Element explored sincerity with a *descriptive* eye (attempting to understand what it is to be sincere and insincere), the second half will cover the *normative* aspects of sincerity: what sincerity demands, and what makes it valuable. Our analysis of these concepts will now help us better understand how sincerity governs speech, and why it matters in our society.

3 The Normative Dimension of Sincerity

I have often considered whence this custom that we so religiously observe should spring ... that it should be the highest insult that can in words be done us to reproach us with a lie. Upon examination, I find that it is natural most to defend the defects with which we are most tainted. It seems as if by resenting and being moved at the accusation, we in some sort acquit ourselves of the fault; though we have it in effect, we condemn it in outward appearance.

Montaigne, *Essays, 2, XVIII (On Calling Out Lies)*

3.1 The Norm of Sincerity

From a merely descriptive point of view, sincerity is just a property of utterances. Understood as a norm, instead, it is an expectation or obligation that is placed on the act of uttering a statement. In its most general form, the norm of sincerity simply requires speakers to be sincere:[57]

NORM OF SINCERITY (GENERAL)
One must: make an assertion A only if A is sincere.

However, we saw that sincerity can be understood in different ways. Depending on what 'sincere' is taken to mean, this norm imposes different injunctions. So, for instance, by plugging the intentional expression account into the general formula, we obtain:

NORM OF SINCERITY (INTENTIONAL EXPRESSION)
One must: assert that p only if one thereby intends to express a proposition one believes to be true.

---

[57] The norm could also be construed as a norm demanding no insincerity (along the lines of Grice's First Maxim of Quality; cf. Grice 1989, ch. 2). Due to limitations of space, I won't discuss this variant. For similar reasons, I am also limiting the discussion to *assertoric* sincerity. Finally, it might be doubted that sincerity expectations admit a precise, univocal formulation. Saul (2024, 137) emphasises how dishonest communicators can exploit this normative uncertainty to their advantage – for instance, uncertainty as to whether the norm demands bound or unbound sincerity.

There are as many readings of the general rule as there are conceptions of sincerity. Here's a hearer-centred example:

NORM OF SINCERITY (DECEPTIVE HEARER-CENTRED)
One must: make an assertion A only if one doesn't intend A to deceive one's audience.

In what follows, unless otherwise specified, I will use 'norm of sincerity' to refer to the general formulation, to keep discussion neutral and compatible with each conception of sincerity.

As for the source of sincerity's normativity, scholars disagree, along divisions that almost invariably reflect some disciplinary bias. Moral philosophers tend to emphasise that sincerity is a *moral* norm, like the duty not to harm others. Linguists and philosophers of language typically take for granted that it is a linguistic norm, and specifically a *pragmatic* norm – like a Gricean maxim, or an Austinian felicity condition.[58] Epistemologists will insist that sincerity is an *epistemic* norm; sociologists that it is a *social* norm; and so forth. Despite apparent disagreement, everyone could be right: I lean towards thinking that there's an important sense in which sincerity is a moral norm, an important sense in which it is a linguistic norm, and so forth for its epistemic and social readings.[59]

Our exploration of the normative dimension of sincerity will begin by looking at the complex interactions between sincerity and other norms (Section 3.2). Learning how to solve normative clashes is part of what being a sincere person requires: Section 3.3 provides a cursory overview of philosophical work on sincerity as a virtue. But why is sincerity deemed so valuable by philosophers? A common argument is that communication, society, and testimonial knowledge could simply not exist without a norm of sincerity (Section 3.4). Having reviewed these ideas, the closing section (Section 3.5) will focus on sincerity's epistemic value, and on whether there are epistemic norms beyond it that govern our assertoric practices.

3.2 Sincerity and Other Norms

Obsequium amicos, veritas odium parit.
(Adulation yields friends, sincerity enemies.)

Terenzio, *Andria (v. 68)*

---

[58] I discussed felicity conditions in Section 2.7.2; Gricean maxims are presented in the next section.

[59] Additionally, these norms could in principle come apart: for instance, moral sincerity might demand less (or more) than linguistic sincerity.

Taken in isolation, the norm of sincerity offers a recommendation that is almost comically simplistic. Being sincere is the right thing to do, and we should always be sincere. If only life was that easy! Experience teaches us that reality is more complicated: our best intentions to tell the truth are often shattered by the constraints imposed on us by the circumstances of life.

Simplifying a bit, there are two main obstacles that stand in the way of our best intentions. First, being sincere can clash with personal *interests* (what we *want* to do). In these cases, there is no question that being sincere is (ceteris paribus) the right thing to do – but in some circumstances, the stakes can be high, and sincerity truly costly. Sticking to the norm of sincerity, in this sense, is difficult because it requires sacrificing our preferences on the altar of virtue.

Second, and more interestingly, being sincere can clash with other norms (what we *ought* to do). The locus classicus is Kant's (1797) example of an axe-wielding murderer who inquires whether 'our friend who is pursued by him had taken refuge in our house'.[60] Famously, Kant argued that our duty not to lie is perfect (i.e. exceptionless), and that lying is therefore never permissible – not in such extreme circumstances, and even less so in more mundane cases, where no life is at stake.

Kant defends an 'absolutist' take on the permissibility of lying. No normative clash between one's duty not to lie and other norms should ever be resolved by allowing the speaker to speak insincerely: not even saving a man's life can justify lying. The absolutist view has a respectable philosophical pedigree, with sophisticated arguments in its defence put forward by influential thinkers such as Augustine, Aquinas, and Kant.[61] Despite its sustained influence, however, absolutism has now gone out of fashion: for most contemporary approaches, normative clashes can permissibly be resolved against sincerity – meaning that lying is sometimes justified. These views then disagree on which considerations warrant exceptions (see Carson 2018) – a notoriously difficult task as one moves from life-saving scenarios to more mundane circumstances.[62]

Clashes between sincerity and other norms happen more often than one might realise. A common clash with altruistic considerations happens when an interlocutor solicits information that would harm or hurt them. 'Sticks and stones may break my bones, but words will never hurt me', the refrain goes. But the proverb seems misguided, as words can be very painful – especially when they

---

[60] An analogous case (from Augustine) was discussed in Section 2.3.1: in Two Roads, Marcellus had to choose between an altruistic untruth (which would save Simplicius) or a sincere statement which would send him into the arms of the bandits. In his work, Augustine considers more such clashes, anticipating Kant's discussion.

[61] My succinct presentation of absolutism surely doesn't do justice to these views, which are more nuanced. For discussion, Korsgaard 1986; Sedgwick 1991; Griffiths 2004; Mahon 2006.

[62] For a promising solution, Stokke (2017).

are truthful. Questions like 'Did you like my gift?' 'Do you think he/she really loves me?' or 'How many days do I have left?' might elicit painful truths. Sincerity earned the nickname 'cruel virtue' (Tagliapietra 2003) precisely because being sincere often requires revealing to our interlocutor truths that can hurt. Navigating the narrow space between cruelty and insincerity, accordingly, is sometimes an arduous task.

We saw that sincerity can be understood as both a moral and a linguistic rule.[63] Correspondingly, sincerity can also clash with pragmatic norms on top of moral norms. For example, Grice (1989) argues that conversations are governed by a Maxim of Quantity, which dictates:

1. *Make your contribution as informative as is required (for the current purposes of the exchange).*
2. *Do not make your contribution more informative than is required.*

Sometimes, to follow this norm, we approximate and engage in *loose talk* at the expense of precision and sincerity. Consider the following examples (inspired by Wilson and Sperber 2002):

(1) It's three twenty.
(2) Holland is flat.
(3) I will run to the shop before it closes.

It can be perfectly fine to utter (1–3), even if the speaker believes their content to be literally false. I can appropriately state (1) even if I'm aware that it's not yet 3:20 (e.g. if it's 3:18), (2) even if I'm aware that Holland has some hills and depressions, and (3) even if my plan is to rush to the shop without actually running.

According to Grice, in such cases the speaker is violating the norm of sincerity (the 'Maxim of Quality', in Grice's parlance) in order to follow the Maxim of Quantity. However, unlike in genuine insincerity, where the speaker *covertly* violates the norm, here the violation is *overt* and transparent: the hearer is meant to realise that the speaker is approximating for the sake of simplicity, and that their goal is to communicate *less* than what they literally say – for example, that it is *around* three twenty, or that Holland is *mostly* flat (cf. Hoek 2018).[64]

---

[63] Due to limitations of space, I won't be able to discuss other common clashes, such as clashes with professional or institutional duties. See Bok 1978 for discussion of these intricate issues.

[64] Relevance theorists agree that this is the message to be recovered, but draw a more radical conclusion: that sincerity is subordinate to another pragmatic norm – *relevance* – which demands that speakers only communicate salient content (i.e. content that is worth the audience's processing effort; Wilson 1995; Wilson and Sperber 2002; for an alternative treatment of these cases, see Lasersohn 1999 and the rich literature it inspired).

It's not even clear that overt violations of sincerity like (1–3) constitute genuine violations. For speaker-centred views, the insincere speaker must *express* the believed-false proposition, which requires representing themselves as believing its content. But (2) presumably is meant to represent the speaker as believing that Holland is *mostly* flat, rather than a perfectly flat surface – to interpret the utterance otherwise would be to deliberately misunderstand it. Similarly, so long as the speaker of (2) isn't trying to convince their interlocutor that there are no hills or depressions whatsoever in Holland, hearer-centred standards won't classify their utterance as insincere.[65]

Metaphors and irony behave similarly to *loose talk*: by openly violating expectations of sincerity (*flouting* them, in Grice's parlance) the speaker manifestly intends to convey a true proposition, instead of the literal content of their utterance. This is exemplified by (4) and (5) below, which respectively communicate that the math problem is easy (rather than a confection) and that the speaker is *not* a Taylor Swift fan:[66]

(4) That math problem is a piece of cake
(5) Oh, sure, I'm a Swiftie . . . big time!

A similar phenomenon occurs when sincerity clashes with norms of politeness. When there's mutual awareness that politeness clashes with sincerity, this can affect what we ultimately take the speaker to communicate. Consider the following:

(6) [Peter]: How are you?
(7) [Lewis]: I'm fine.

If Peter and Lewis are, say, barely acquainted business competitors, there is no expectation that Lewis respond to (6) with anything else but (7): bringing up their personal life's difficulties would be socially inappropriate. Similarly, an expression like (8) is often expected regardless of whether the speaker genuinely feels happy about the achievements of the recipient.

(8) Congratulations!

Given that politeness demands the use of these expressions even in the absence of the mental state that they supposedly express,[67] we don't always

---

[65] For ALETHIC PROXIMITY, (1–3) are even more straightforwardly sincere, since they don't stray too far from what the speaker considers true.

[66] If the speaker does not believe that the problem is easy, or if they do like Taylor Swift, (4–5) can still be insincere. This is acknowledged by all unbound definitions, and discussed in contemporary literature under the label of 'non-literal lying' (Viebahn 2021; Marsili and Löhr 2022; Güngör 2024).

[67] Or that they supposedly aim to induce in the audience, if you're a manipulation-theorist.

take them to communicate these states. By uttering them, the speaker often conforms to a social ritual (like saying 'Hello!' or 'Goodbye!') without communicating much, beyond their willingness to conform to that ritual. If this is right, at least *some* polite falsities aren't truly insincere, because no believed-false content is asserted or otherwise communicated (cf. Nagel 1998). Which is not to say, of course, that polite falsities can never be insincere or genuinely mendacious. Consider the classic:

(9) You look soooooo good with your new haircut!

Presumably, polite falsities like (9) rather lean towards the insincerity end of the scale – especially if volunteered by the speaker, rather than elicited by a question. In other cases, weighing politeness against sincerity is more difficult, yielding mixed verdicts. Adjudication will depend on what we know about the speaker's intentions: the clearer it is whether the speaker intends to present the believed-false content as true, the clearer the verdict about each case.

3.3 Sincerity as a Virtue, Insincerity as a Vice

I mentioned (Section 2.1.1) that sincerity can be understood both as a *property of utterances* ('discursive sincerity', our focus so far) and as a *property of speakers* ('dispositional sincerity'). The two notions, of course, are related. A sincere person is a person who has a stable disposition to make sincere statements. If the virtue of sincerity amounts to having this disposition, this opens up some different ways of understanding it, depending on what 'sincerity' is taken to mean. For example, on the simplest speaker-centred view, this is what sincerity demands:

> Speaker-centred virtue of sincerity
> *A sincere person is one with a stable disposition to only assert what they believe to be true.*

Interestingly, different accounts of sincerity could be regarded not as competing theories, but as different ways in which a virtuous speaker might excel. A sincere speaker should strive to be precise (Alethic Proximity), calibrate confidence to certainty (Comparative), be mindful of the effect of their statements on the audience (hearer-centred sincerity), and so forth. Each descriptive account of sincerity, then, yields a different insight on its normative profile: what it demands as a virtue, and why it is valuable.

What about the vice of insincerity? Despite growing interest in vice epistemology, I'm not aware of any systematic discussion of this vice: insincerity is often listed next to other vices, but not discussed.[68] Let's try to fill this gap. It's tempting to define the vice as the mirror image of the virtue, simply switching 'true' for 'false' in the schema. However, only pathological liars have a stable disposition to only assert disbelieved propositions. A more promising alternative is to understand the vice of insincerity as the absence of the virtue of sincerity. The resulting conception rings more plausible:

> SPEAKER-CENTRED VICE OF INSINCERITY
> *An insincere person is one without a stable disposition to only assert what they believe to be true.*

Virtue theorists (in ethics and epistemology) sometimes emphasise that being virtuous requires valuing virtuous conduct (like sincerity) as intrinsically desirable. Norms like the norm of sincerity, by contrast, are often taken to be sustained by an infrastructure of social policing: speakers are motivated to be sincere because infractions are socially sanctioned. To be motivated by such instrumental considerations, some argue, falls short of possessing the virtue of sincerity. For Williams (2002, 59), the truly sincere person is disposed to be sincere not because sincerity has instrumental value (e.g. in preserving one's reputation), but because they recognise sincerity as intrinsically right and desirable. The virtue of sincerity, on this view, also requires being moved by a genuine appreciation of the worth of being sincere.

Philosophical reflection on the virtue of sincerity has deep historical roots. Aristotle's *Nicomachean Ethics* laid important groundwork. For Aristotle, the sincere person (*aletheutikos*) embodies a mean (*mesotes*) between two vicious extremes: the boastful exaggeration of the braggart and the sly dissimulation of the self-deprecator. Aristotle's discussion focuses on authentic self-presentation and discourse *about oneself* (Curzer 2012, ch. 10). The sincere person speaks the truth about who they are, no more and no less than what one deserves (NE, IV, 7, 1127a 17–28).

Somewhat unsurprisingly, Aquinas (ST, II-II, 109, a1) aligns with Aristotle's position. Both Aristotle and Aquinas acknowledge that understatements are a lesser threat to sincerity than overstatements. After all, the boaster generally gains undeserved credit, whereas the modest speaker avoids ostentation, as Socrates himself did (NE IV, 7, 1127b 25–26). Additionally, understating can be 'done without prejudice to truth, since the lesser is contained in the greater' (ST II-II, 109, a4). Contemporary work agrees on this point: as assertoric force increases (as in stronger, boosted statements), the same communicated content

---

[68] Some attention has been directed to the related vice of epistemic insouciance – a 'lack of concern about the facts or an indifference to whether [one's] beliefs and statements have any basis in reality', whose 'primary product' is bullshit (Cassam 2018, 2–3).

is, ceteris paribus, more insincere (Marsili 2014; 2018a). Excessive modesty (including understatement), however, is also seen as a vice by some philosophers, and receives the highest condemnation from Montaigne (*Essays*, 2, XVII):

> *As to this new virtue of feigning and dissimulation, which is now in so great credit, I mortally hate it; and of all vices find none that evidences so much baseness and meanness of spirit. 'Tis a cowardly and servile humour to hide and disguise a man's self under a visor, and not to dare to show himself what he is.*

A separate issue is whether sincerity, as a virtue, requires a disposition to *disclose* one's beliefs. Some philosophers hold the strong view that the truly virtuous speaker has to be *supersincere* (Section 2.1.2). Rousseau's (RSW) radical take, for example, is that sincerity requires full transparency, including volunteering information that jeopardises one's reputation and social standing.[69] Although Rousseau is somewhat an outlier, some contemporary philosophers (Williams 2002, ch. 5; Queloz 2021, 165–66) think that the virtue of sincerity is incompatible with deliberately withholding information, and demands speaking up at least under some circumstances, such as when disclosure is socially expected or helpful.

I have already stated my (mainly terminological) case against this view. If our concern is *sincerity in discourse*, sincerity cannot impose demands on what one has not yet said. So understood, then, sincerity merely requires that *when* something is communicated (explicitly or indirectly), it matches one's belief. Observing this dictum is generally compatible with omission and dissimulation. To put it in Montaigne's words: 'A man must not always tell all, for that were folly: but what a man says should be what he thinks, otherwise 'tis knavery' (*Essays*, 2, XVII).

This is not to deny that supersincerity might be demanded by other virtues. *Spontaneity* (though not necessarily a virtue) is a disposition to telling immediately and directly what you believe – a disposition to share one's thoughts in an unmediated way. *Frankness* is often understood as a disposition to disclose hard truths – even those that can hurt the interlocutor, or that might clash with social expectations. The courageous revelation of hard truths is also required by *parrhesia*, a disposition (famously discussed by Foucault 2011) to speak the truth, especially against repression and silencing by oppressive authorities. Spontaneity, frankness, and parrhesia all require some degree of supersincerity, since they demand voluntary disclosure of information – often, information that the speaker would profit from keeping to themselves.

---

[69] For a critical discussion of Rousseau's take on sincerity, see Williams 2002 (ch.8).

Is sincerity the manifestation of some other more general virtue? For Miller (2021, 22–23), sincerity should be understood as a form of honesty.[70] He characterises honesty as a general disposition to act in a way that doesn't intentionally distort the facts as the agent sees them. For instance, a cheater typically misrepresents the facts about whether they are following the relevant rules. They are dishonest, but not insincere (insofar as their cheating doesn't involve communicating insincerely). If this is right, then the misrepresentation of facts, which some might intuitively regard as the hallmark of insincerity, is central to all dishonest behaviour. Sincerity, in turn, might be regarded as the manifestation of honesty in speech – a disposition *to communicate* in a way that doesn't intentionally distort the facts as the agent sees them.

3.4 Sincerity: Language, Knowledge, and Society

Philosophers hold sincerity in high regard. They often depict it as a fundamental virtue, or an exceptionless norm, lying at the foundations of human morality. Why is sincerity considered so important and valuable? What purpose does it serve in our society? Let's review some answers, focusing on sincerity's role in sustaining communication (Sections 3.4.1–2), meaningful social relationships (Section 3.4.3), and testimony (Section 3.5).

3.4.1 Sincerity as the Foundation of Communication

Could there be a linguistic community where people are insincere virtually all the time, but still manage to communicate? Coady (1992) imagines an alien world of this sort, where individuals never speak the truth – let's call this planet Lars (like Mars, but with an L for lying):

> LARS
>
> *Let us suppose for the moment that [the Lartians] have a language which we can translate (there are difficulties in this supposition as we shall see shortly) with names for distinguishable things in their environment and suitable predicative equipment. We find however, to our astonishment, that whenever they construct sentences addressed to each other in the absence (from their vicinity) of the things designated by the names ... then they seem to say what we (more synoptically placed) can observe to be false.*

Can we really say that the Lartians (the inhabitants of Lars) have a practice of *asserting*, or of *reporting* what happens in the external world? Let's assume that expressing a belief is essential to communication and assertion, in the spirit of

---

[70] Miller uses a slightly different vocabulary: 'truthfulness' indicates the speaker-centred virtue of sincerity, 'forthrightness' its non-literal counterpart, and 'veracity' covers both (minor details aside).

'expression theories'. Since no correlation between the speaker's assertions and their beliefs is ever observed on Lars, it's hard to see how assertions could be regarded as devices for expressing beliefs. By expression-theoretic standards, then, no genuine assertions can be made on Lars. A similar conclusion follows from contagion views. On Lars, the function of assertions cannot be to persuade audiences: given that their statements are never observed to match reality, Lartian speakers cannot be intending to persuade even the most gullible of audiences. Whatever Lartians are doing with declarative sentences, it's something different from our practice of asserting.[71]

Widespread insincerity also threatens to break down the smaller components of language: the meaning of nouns and predicates. If a word like 'walrus' refers to a certain category of mammals, it's not because this string of letters has some intrinsic relation with the marine species. Rather, it's because our linguistic community established a convention, and English speakers coordinate to use the term in this way. It's hard to imagine how such coordination could be achieved on LARS. When a walrus is present, Lartians will indicate it and proffer all sorts of unrelated expressions: things like 'That's a boat!', or 'That's Henry Kissinger!' In virtue of what would words have the meaning they have in LARS? Coady (83–89) is highly sceptical that we can come up with a plausible theory of meaning that addresses this question.

For similar reasons, language acquisition would be practically impossible. Lartian children will hear all sort of things when they're around walruses: adults will indicate the animal and call it a boat, Henry Kissinger, and all sorts of other things. If language acquisition requires repeated exposure to regularities, and a language without sincerity breaks down these regularities, then language acquisition isn't possible – or at least very difficult – on Lars.

Thought experiments like LARS seem to demonstrate that without a modicum of sincerity, no meaningful linguistic communication can occur[72]. Some philosophers take this idea further. In 'Languages and Language' (1975), Lewis (building on Stenius 1967) argues that truthfulness and trust are essential to linguistic communication. For Lewis, to have a language at all just is to have such a convention:[73]

---

[71] The same conclusion is reached also by the orthodox view (cf. Marsili and Green 2021, 23–26) that asserting requires *presenting a proposition as true*. Since no correlation can ever be observed between statements and reality on Lars, Lartians could hardly see themselves as being in the business of presenting the content of their utterances as descriptions of the world.

[72] For a different take, see Skyrms 2010 (73–82).

[73] Conventions are understood by Lewis as arbitrary, self-sustaining solutions to coordination problems (for a full definition, Lewis 1975, 4–7).

> *My proposal is that the convention whereby a population P uses a language £
> is a convention of truthfulness and trust in £. To be truthful in £ is to act in a
> certain way: to try never to utter any sentences of £ that are not true in £.Thus
> it is to avoid uttering any sentence of £ unless one believes it to be true in £. To
> be trusting in £ is to form beliefs in a certain way: to impute truthfulness in £
> to others, and thus to tend to respond to another's utterance of any sentence of
> £ by coming to believe that the uttered sentence is true in £. (7; my emphasis)*

On this view, linguistic communication is made possible by a convention that speakers try to make assertions that are true (truthfulness), so that hearers generally interpret assertions as true (trust). This enables coordination between communicators. Unlike Coady's Lartians, the Lewisian 'population P' experiences a regular (albeit not perfect) correspondence between what people say and states of the world, so that none of the Lartian difficulties (in language acquisition, interpretation, etc.) arise.

Grice (1989, 27) also regards sincerity[74] as a prerequisite for meaningful communication. In his 'Retrospective Epilogue' he emphasises that unless expectations of sincerity (in his terminology, 'the maxim of Quality') are in place, utterances fail to be genuinely communicative (in his terminology, 'contributions'):

> *The maxim of Quality, enjoining the provision of contributions which are
> genuine rather than spurious (truthful rather than mendacious), does not
> seem to be just one among a number of recipes for producing contributions; it
> seems rather to spell out the difference between something's being and
> (strictly speaking) failing to be, any kind of contribution at all. (371)*

3.4.2 When Insincerity Spreads

Some philosophers took this line of reasoning even further. For Immanuel Kant, sincerity is an unconditional duty that is essential not only for meaningful language use but also for the very existence of modern society. Kant goes so far as to suggest that every single lie threatens the collapse of language and of institutions (Kant 1797, 8:426):

> *[When I lie,] I cause that declarations should in general find no credence, and
> hence that all rights based on contracts should be void and lose their force,
> and this is a wrong done to mankind generally.*

---

[74] To be precise, both Lewis's and Grice's discussions oscillate between two notions: the speaker-centred norm of sincerity, and the requirement that the speaker should *aim (or try) to tell the truth*. Lewis's definition of truthfulness appeals to the latter, but immediately specifies that it entails the former (see my emphasis in the quoted text). Grice has different labels for the former notion ('First Maxim of Quality') and the latter ('Supermaxim of Quality'); though ambiguous, the passage I am about to discuss seems to focus on the former.

Taken literally, Kant's position comes across as bizarrely radical: how can a single lie have such profound consequences on the fabric of society? But his remarks point in the direction of two plausible claims. The first is that lies pose an incremental threat to the credibility of assertions: the more lying spreads in a population, the less credible each assertion made by an individual who belongs to that population.[75] The second is that sincerity matters not only for communication but for society at large. The point is familiar at least since Aquinas's *Summa Theologiae*:

> *Since man is a social animal, one man naturally owes another whatever is necessary for the preservation of human society. Now it would be impossible for men to live together, unless they believed one another, as declaring the truth one to another. (ST, II, II, a. 3 ad 1)*

If Aquinas is right, a functioning society requires a modicum of interpersonal trust, and that trust is difficult to achieve if one cannot expect other people to be sincere. Sincerity, then, is a conditio sine qua non for human civilisation. Modern societies rely on communication and mutual trust to create complex networks of obligations. Institutions and social objects (nations, money, corporations, contracts) all rely on the presumption that people, by and large, do what they say they will. Without sincerity and loyalty (as defined in Section 2.7.2), there can be no functioning society.

3.4.3 Sincerity and Knowledge

There's another human faculty that presumably depends on sincerity: our ability to learn from testimony. There's no doubt that much of human knowledge has been passed on through communication, rather than by direct acquaintance with the known facts (Coady 1992; Alfano and Levy 2020). In the late 1980s, philosophers grew increasingly interested in the importance of *testimony*. 'Testimony' here designates any speech act that presents a proposition as true,[76] typically to persuade an interlocutor. Testimonial beliefs, in turn, are beliefs acquired by accepting testimony.

Historically, philosophers have been disagreeing about the conditions under which testimonial beliefs can be said to be *warranted*, or to amount to

---

[75] This idea has been well explored in the game-theoretic literature, where mathematical models are adopted to study how the spread of deceptive signallers threatens to undermine a population's ability to communicate meaningfully (Skyrms 2010). The conclusions of these studies, however, are less dire than Kant's: a communicative system can retain stability (in a game-theoretic sense) despite widespread deception, and senders can successfully convey information even when deception is universal (Skyrms 2010, 73–82).

[76] This characterisation will inevitably find detractors, but it is sufficiently general for current purposes. On defining testimony, see Lackey 2006 and Cullison 2010.

knowledge.[77] Most theorists, however, would agree that sincerity is an important prerequisite for our ability to acquire testimonial knowledge. In Coady's Lartian society, where expectations of sincerity are absent, testimonial knowledge is surely beyond reach: if Lartians were able to communicate, they certainly could not trust the reports of their fellows.

Let's grant that we can learn through testimony, and that this is at least in part because this process of information acquisition, in combination with other cognitive faculties,[78] is sufficiently reliable. Two questions then remain open: Which role does sincerity play in our ability to acquire testimonial knowledge? And is sincerity all we demand from testimony?

3.5 Testimony and the Norm of Sincerity

3.5.1 Testimony and Epistemic Norms

Philosophers often emphasise the importance of *epistemic norms* (and obligations) in sustaining the reliability of testimony. In a nutshell, if a good proportion of testimony is veridical, it's because (some argue) communicators keep each other in check, ensuring that veridical testimony gets rewarded, and unreliable testimony punished (Williams 2002; Goldberg 2011; 2015; Marsili forth). Much contemporary work in epistemology aims to uncover which epistemic norms govern testimonial communication, and how they exceed expectations of sincerity (if they do).

Since Williamson (1996), philosophical discussion of epistemic norms generally accepts some foundational assumptions. Assertion is allegedly governed by a *single* norm of the form 'Assert that p only if p has C', where C is an epistemic property (such as *knowledge* or *justification*). Unlike norms of politeness, or other conversational norms (such as the Gricean Maxims of Quantity discussed in Section 3.2), the norm of assertion regulates *only* the speech act of assertion – it is distinctive of it. If these simplifying assumptions are granted,[79] identifying the norm of assertion is a matter of determining which single property makes a proposition assertable (i.e. epistemically permissible to assert). The following proposals dominate the debate:

---

[77] *Non-reductionists*, who hold that we have a pro tanto epistemic entitlement to trust (a piece of) testimony, oppose *reductionists,* who deny that we have such an epistemic entitlement. (For an introduction, see Leonard 2023). Crucially, both agree that trusting testimony *under the right conditions* yields knowledge.

[78] This qualification includes *epistemic vigilance* (our ability to assess sources for their reliability, and content for its plausibility, Sperber et al. 2010), making the claim compatible with both reductionism and non-reductionism.

[79] For a review of reasons not to accept them, see Pagin and Marsili 2021 (Supplementary Document: Which Kind of Norm?).

KNOWLEDGE-RULE (KR): *Assert p only if you know that p.*

TRUTH-RULE (TR): *Assert p only if p is true.*

JUSTIFICATION-RULE (JR): *Assert p only if you rationally believe that p.*

BELIEF-RULE (BR): *Assert p only if you believe that p.*[80]

Typically, defenders of more demanding norms (like KR, JR, or TR) acknowledge that speakers are expected to conform to a sincerity-rule like BR.[81] However, there are exceptions: it has been argued that BR *doesn't* regulate assertion, and that we could count on testimony to be reliable even in its absence. The next section presents and tackles these objections. After establishing that BR is *necessary* for permissible assertion, we'll deal with its *sufficiency*: whether the norm of assertion is, in fact, more stringent than this sincerity norm.

3.5.2 Against Sincerity: Selfless Assertions

According to BR, the belief-rule, an assertion is epistemically permissible only if it's believed to be true. This belief-rule is effectively a sincerity-rule, since it says that an assertion is appropriate only if it is sincere in the speaker-centred sense.[82]

Philosophers rarely question the idea that BR governs assertoric speech. After all, 'Don't lie' is one of the first communicative rules that we learn as we begin to speak. Expectations of sincerity are so engrained that we tend to take them for granted, both in life and in philosophical theorising. But not all philosophers agree that they are universal.

The most prominent critic of BR is Jennifer Lackey, who argues that justification, but not belief, is required for appropriate assertion. She defends the following variant of JR:

EXTERNAL-JUSTIFICATION-RULE (JR*): *Assert p only if it is rational for you to believe that p.*

---

[80] This list is inevitably not exhaustive, and it contains significant approximations. It groups together importantly different views (such as *justification-rules*, which differ radically from one another). It also leaves out many prominent alternative views, like the context-sensitive proposal defended by Goldberg (2015). For a more detailed review, see Pagin and Marsili 2021.

[81] Since you can only know what you believe, KR requires conformity to BR. JR is often understood by its proponents to require reasonable or justified belief. The story is more complicated for TR, which is said to require belief via 'secondary norms', because conformity to a norm allegedly requires that you reasonably believe that you are following the norm (Weiner 2005; Whiting 2012). For criticism of this move, see footnote 93.

[82] Contagion views, too, can be linked to BR. If you try to get your audience to believe what you assert, then cooperation demands that you only assert propositions that you believe. This is the familiar Gricean picture, and Bach (2008) defends BR precisely by appealing to this principle.

The idea underlying this proposal is that speakers should strive to assert not what they personally believe is true, but rather propositions that are well supported by the evidence (regardless of their own doxastic commitments).

Of course, JR* and BR often converge in their predictions: if it is rational for me to believe that p, I will often believe that p. But what about those cases when justification and belief come apart, and a speaker fails to believe what they are justified in believing? For Lackey (2007), it is precisely in these cases that we can notice the superiority of JR*. Only this rule can accommodate the intuitive appropriateness of *selfless assertions*, which she defines as follows:

> *An assertion that p is selfless if and only if:*
> 1. *a subject, for purely non-epistemic reasons, doesn't believe that p;*
> 2. *despite this lack of belief, the subject is aware that p is very well supported by all of the available evidence; and*
> 3. *because of this, the subject asserts that p without believing that p. (599; substantially edited)*

The most widely discussed example of selfless assertion involves a doxastic conflict between religious faith and scientific evidence (Lackey 2007):

CREATIONIST TEACHER
Stella, a creationist teacher, is aware that evolutionary theory is supported by the best available evidence, but firmly accepts creationism (which contradicts evolutionary theory) on the basis of her religious faith. Suppose that Stella tells her students (10), which she believes to be false:

(10) Homo sapiens *evolved from* Homo erectus.

Intuitively, it would be appropriate for Stella, as a teacher, to assert (10): after all, she is presenting what she takes to be the scientific consensus on the subject. In a classroom context, this seems appropriate. But BR predicts that (10), a believed-false statement, should come across as inappropriate and worthy of criticism. Generalising, the intuitive appropriateness of selfless assertion challenges the universality of (speaker-centred[83]) expectations of sincerity, and appears to corroborate Lackey's view that speakers are only expected to make justified assertions, regardless of whether they believe them.

However, there are several considerations that should give us pause. First, it's doubtful whether selfless assertions are genuine assertions. Teachers are under a professional obligation to teach students the scientific consensus, not their personal opinions. In this light, utterances like (10) could be understood as speech acts that

---

[83] It could be argued that Stella is not aiming to get her students to believe that she personally believes (10) to be true, and that selfless assertors lack this sort of hearer-centred insincere intention more generally.

fall short of assertion (e.g. an act of *reporting* the theories that are presented in the book) or as assertions with implicitly prefaced contents ('*According to the scientific consensus*, (10)'). Under both interpretations, Stella's utterance would not be insincere, nor would it prove that there are permissible violations of BR and KR. It has been argued (Milić 2017) that this treatment extends to other examples discussed in the literature, too, since they involve statements made under professional obligation (e.g. by a vaccine-sceptical *doctor*, a racist *juror*).

In response, for each scenario, one might imagine the speaker repeating the same statement in a different, informal context – talking to a friend at the pub, for instance (Lackey 2007, 601). However, once we move to non-professional contexts, intuitions about the appropriateness of the statement change. Imagine that Stella asserts (10), without any qualification, to a childhood friend in a pub. Here there's a stronger case to be made that Stella is lying, or at least that her assertion is defective in important ways – she is, after all, falsely presenting the scientific consensus as her own opinion, without any qualification (cf. Milić 2017, 2291–93).

Relatedly, if one accepts that selfless assertions are genuine assertions, it's unclear whether they are appropriate. Selfless assertors always have the option to use fuller, more informative expressions. For example:

(11)   According to the available evidence, p. But if you are asking me what I think, not-p.

By choosing the unqualified assertion (p) over more informative expressions like (11), selfless assertors misrepresent themselves as believing what they do not actually believe. They imply (or at least let the audience infer) that they believe what they are saying, thereby letting their audience form a false belief, when this is perfectly avoidable – given the availability of (11). By most unbound standards, (10) is therefore insincere. While Lackey insists that an evidence-based assertion (rather than one reflecting personal, unfounded beliefs) is what the audience expects (2007, 117–18), this overlooks that in informal contexts, where conversational goals standardly include sharing and comparing opinions, choosing (10) over (11) is misleading. Accordingly, there is an important sense in which the assertion is defective, criticisable, or even epistemically impermissible (given the available alternatives).[84]

---

[84] In fact, the verdict that Stella's assertion should feel defective (in informal contexts, at least) seems inescapable given Lackey's own framework, since she argues that communication is governed by NMNA** ('S should assert that p in context C only if it is not reasonable for S to believe that the assertion that p will be misleading in C relative to the purposes of the exchange in question') in addition to JR*. In non-professional contexts, the purposes of exchange standardly include sharing and comparing opinions, and violations of NMNA should be intuitively inappropriate in her view. So, Lackey has to drop either the claim that selfless assertions are intuitively appropriate or the claim that NMNA** governs all conversational exchanges.

Suppose you have the opposite intuition. Stella is aware that (10) has good epistemic credentials, and that it's therefore likely to be true: intuitively, then, her assertion is permissible. Empirical evidence (Turri 2014) shows that many non-philosophers share this opinion. However, the same study found that when participants judge a selfless assertion permissible, they almost invariably interpret the scenario as one in which the protagonist believes that what they are asserting is true. In other words, when people feel the pull of the intuition that (10) is appropriate, it's typically because they regard Stella's awareness of the evidence in support of (10) as an indicator that she actually believes that (10) is true. Our intuitions about selfless assertions, in other words, get polluted by our instinctive tendency to ascribe belief to agents who *should* form that belief, given their evidence base. This should give us pause before we draw strong theoretical conclusions from intuitions about these scenarios.

In conclusion, selfless assertions are too controversial to serve as decisive counterexamples. They're complex scenarios, whose interpretation is debatable. It's not clear that they are genuine (unqualified) assertions. It's not clear that they are intuitively appropriate. And it's not clear that our intuitions about them aren't polluted by some natural propensity to ascribe beliefs to the speaker as if they were thinking rationally. Before abandoning the strongly intuitive thesis that assertions are governed by a sincerity norm, compelling evidence is needed. While selfless assertions complicate the picture, they don't provide the knockout argument that we'd need to abandon the consensus view that there is a pro tanto expectation that people believe what they assert.[85]

3.5.3 Unjustified Beliefs and Assertions

To accept that assertions are governed by BR is not yet to agree that BR is the *only* epistemic requirement for proper assertion. In fact, this is an unpopular view, since assertions can be epistemically faulty even when they are sincere. Sometimes people form beliefs on very poor grounds – a hunch, wishful thinking, fallacious inferences, and so on. Let's call such poorly formed beliefs 'unjustified beliefs', to emphasise that they are not supported by appropriate evidence or reasons. When speakers assert such beliefs without qualification, they make *unjustified assertions*. In most contexts, such assertions are epistemically faulty. Consider the following case:

GOOD COOK
Bob and Rachel are having a conversation about their common friend Jacques. Rachel asks whether Jacques is a good cook. Bob does not know.

---

[85] For some additional considerations against BR, see Wilson 1995; Wilson and Sperber 2002; Mandelkern and Dorst 2022.

> *However, Bob knows that Jacques is French, and he is under the impression*
> *that French people are often excellent cooks. On this basis, he replies:*
>
> *(12) Sure, Jacques is an excellent cook.*

In asserting (12), Bob makes an *unjustified assertion*. Intuitively, (12) is epistemically inappropriate[86] – presumably, because Bob lacks sufficient ground to make his claim. Imagine that you later realise that Bob had no evidence for (12) beyond Jacques's nationality. It would be natural (and appropriate) for you to complain, or to criticise Bob for his unfounded claim. More generally: unjustified assertions are inappropriate, and BR alone cannot accommodate this fact. This limitation is equally acknowledged in epistemology and pragmatics. Grice's (1989) Second Maxim of Quality dictates that cooperative communication requires appropriate evidence in addition to sincerity (cf. Searle 1969, 66). Most epistemologist, too, argue that assertion is governed by a stricter rule (like JR or KR) and underscore the impermissibility of unjustified assertions.

3.5.4 The Compound View

The shortcomings of BR can be addressed by pairing it with a norm that forbids the acceptance of unjustified beliefs – this, at least, is the solution propounded by the 'compound view'. This view comes in two flavours, depending on whether the compounding requirement is understood as a *norm of belief* or as an *epistemic virtue*. Let's start with the first.

Bach (2008) and Hindriks (2007) suggest that while assertion is only subject to BR, beliefs are themselves subject to norms – specifically, a norm that demands that one should believe only what one knows.[87] Once this requirement is paired with BR, we get the derivative requirement that one should only assert what one knows. Hindriks (2007, 23) summarises the derivation as follows:[88]

[BR] One must: assert that p only if one believes that p.
[KR-B] One must: believe that p only if one knows that p.
∴ [KR] One must: assert that p only if one knows that p.

If KR can be derived from BR, unjustified assertions are forbidden, reconciling BR with our intuitions.

---

[86] The intuition that UNJUSTIFIED ASSERTIONS are inappropriate is cross-cultural, robust, and widespread (Kneer 2021, Graham and Pedersen 2024, Kneer and Marsili 2025).

[87] Whether this claim is plausible is itself a matter of controversy (McGlynn 2014; Hughes 2017).

[88] I altered the acronyms to match the ones I adopt. Additionally, Hindriks qualifies BR and KR so that they hold only 'in situations of normal trust'.

Prior to Bach and Hindriks, Williams (2002) defended a version of the compound view articulated in terms of virtues, rather than norms. The compounding virtues are *Sincerity* and *Accuracy*. I presented Williams's account of the former earlier (Section 3.3). Accuracy, on the other hand, involves (broadly) a disposition to form beliefs in a careful way. A careful believer displays a sensitivity to evidence, a concern for truth, and a disposition to 'get things right'. Like Bach's or Hindriks's knowledge norm of belief, it ensures that people don't form unjustified beliefs. But there are key differences.

First, Williams's emphasis is on accuracy (and therefore a stable correlation with truth), rather than knowledge. Second, for Williams only a virtue that is valued in its own right can effectively sustain our epistemic practices. Despite these differences, the virtue-theoretic compound view yields a similar picture. The virtue of sincerity ensures that what people assert, by and large, tracks what they believe. In turn, accuracy ensures that what people believe, by and large, tracks the truth. The result is a community in which assertions reliably convey beliefs that are true and justified.

Compound views postulate a normative 'division of labour' between doxastic and assertoric normativity. An *assertoric* norm (or virtue) of sincerity ensures that our claims reliably express beliefs; a *doxastic* norm (or virtue) for belief ensures that our beliefs reliably track the truth. Crucially, this means that BR exhausts assertoric normativity: additional requirements are due to doxastic normativity.

However, compound views face serious objections. First, there is a *derivation objection:* it's not clear that we are entitled to derive KR from KR-B and BR. If assertion requires belief, it doesn't follow that it also requires an *epistemically responsible* belief (unless epistemically responsible belief is what BR really requires – but that would end up conflating it with JR). If this is right, Hindriks's derivation of KR from KR-B is invalid (cf. Simion 2018).

To make matters worse, it can be argued that 'must' refers to an altogether different kind of normativity in [BR] and in [KR-B]. The normative force of assertoric norms is grounded in contingent *social* facts: whether it is enforced in a certain linguistic community (García-Carpintero 2022) that polices its infractions (Alston 2000, 251–62). Not so for norms of belief, which are rather grounded in a priori *epistemic* facts – facts about what it is to believe something, and to do so rationally. If this is right, the Bach-Hindriks derivation relies on deontic equivocation (cf. Simion 2018).

Second, there is a *source objection*. Presumably, if we are entitled to criticise an unjustified assertion, it is not because the speaker has formed an unjustified belief. Recall GOOD COOK. When we say that (12) warrants criticism, we mean that there's something *about the statement* that warrants criticism, rather than something about Bob's beliefs – the latter can be criticised too, but their existence alone does not entitle us to publicly rebuke Bob. If this is right, the compound view mischaracterises what is objectionable about Bob's claim, since it traces the normative reason for our perception of an infraction (and our entitlement to criticise his assertion) to Bob's unjustified belief, rather than his assertion.

3.5.5 The Expansive View

Taken alone, the sincerity-rule doesn't capture what is objectionable about unjustified assertions. This, at least, if sincerity is understood to require speaker-centred sincerity, along BR's lines. But what about more expansive conceptions of insincerity, like unbound conceptions?

In GOOD COOK, Bob doesn't believe that what he claimed is false: he isn't insincere by speaker-centred standards. Unbound hearer-centred conceptions, however, paint a slightly different picture. Bob knows that his statement, though sincere (by speaker-centred standards), will almost certainly cause Rachel to acquire a false belief – for example, the belief that Bob has evidence for his claim (such as having heard or experienced that Jacques is a good cook). In other words, Bob's statement is *knowingly deceptive*, even if it's not *intentionally designed* to deceive. It's debatable whether this is enough to meet the requirements of DECEPTIVE HEARER-CENTRED insincerity; to address this concern, we can introduce a minor tweak:

BROAD DECEPTIVE HEARER-CENTRED
- *An assertion is insincere iff S expects that their assertion will cause A to believe a false proposition.*
- *An assertion is sincere otherwise.*

Turning this definition into a norm, sincerity would be understood not as a duty to say what we believe, but rather as a duty to prevent our statements from causing audiences to acquire false beliefs (cf. Eriksson 2011). The result is an 'expansive' belief-norm of assertion:

(BR'): *One must: assert a proposition p only if one does not expect that one's assertion will cause the audience to believe*[89] *propositions that one believes to be false.*

---

[89] To avoid objections like COOKIES (Section 2.6.2), this clause can be expanded as 'or continue to believe'. BR' is similar to Lackey's NMNA (cf. footnote 84) – although Lackey presents it as a general communicative norm, not as a sincerity-rule.

This is a demanding conception of sincerity, but not a particularly artificial one. An injunction like 'Do your best to avoid deceiving the audience' seems the kind of maxim that a speaker truly committed to sincerity should aim to follow. By this criterion, unjustified assertions like (12) are impermissible, because they knowingly misrepresent the speaker's knowledge base. There is no need to defer this verdict to norms of belief (like compound views do). Bob violates BR' because he is aware (as any competent speaker would be) that he will likely lead Rachel to believe a false proposition (e.g. that he has evidence for his claim).

However, speakers are not always fully aware of what they are doing. If Bob is distracted or careless, he could be completely oblivious to the effects that his statement will have on Rachel. A staunch defender of BR' might insist that in this scenario Bob's (12) would be impeccable, because it isn't expected to cause any epistemic harm. However, if one thinks that sincerity is a duty to ensure that one's assertions don't cause the audience to acquire false beliefs, then Bob's obliviousness by no means displays a truly sincere attitude. BR' would then need to be amended to rule out this option, by requiring that the speaker's expectation not to cause epistemic damage is actually reasonable.

(BR''): *One must: assert a proposition p only if one doesn't expect, with good reasons, that one's assertion will cause the audience to accept propositions that one believes to be false.*

The result is a sort of epistemic 'duty of care' for our assertions' doxastic effects. Speakers are expected to avoid *foreseeable harms* (i.e. avoiding foreseeable – not just intended – deception) and to exhibit *reasonable diligence* (i.e. their expectations need to be reasonable).

The reappearance of a 'reasonableness' requirement might raise the suspicion that BR'' borrows resources from justification-rules (which define assertability in terms of reasonable belief).[90] However, this concern is misplaced. BR'' is a genuine (hearer-centred) sincerity-rule, because it only requires that the speaker aims not to cause a discrepancy between *their beliefs* and the *hearer's beliefs*. There is no requirement that the speaker's belief in their assertion (or in what they indirectly communicate with it) is reasonable. Only the assessment of the assertion's communicative effect on the audience must be reasonable.

A more pressing worry is that BR' and BR'' indirectly assume that speakers invite their audiences to believe that their assertions are supported by evidence. Arguably, only JR can establish this assumption. If no norm like JR governs assertion, it's not obvious why Rachel should be entitled to infer that Bob has evidence in support of (12), leaving BR'-BR'' with no resources to explain

---

[90] A conception of sincerity that explicitly does so is Eriksson's 2011 (231–32).

what's wrong with (12). One might then suspect that these proposals implicitly assume JR, rather than representing an alternative to it.

However, pragmatic principles other than JR can explain why audiences are entitled to this conclusion. Consider the Maxim of Quantity, which dictates that contributions shouldn't be less informative than required by the purpose of the exchange (cf. Section 3.2). If the purpose of the exchange is to establish whether Jacques is a good cook, knowing that Bob's belief is based on a wild conjecture, rather than evidence, is certainly relevant information. Bob's (12) then violates the Maxim of Quantity unless he discloses this information (e.g. by qualifying his statement), which is instrumentally helpful given the purpose of the conversation. This could entitle Rachel to her inference, with no need to appeal to JR.[91]

If the foregoing is on the right track, BR" can explain what is wrong about unjustified assertions without implicitly appealing to JR. For those who want to preserve the idea that sincerity, not justification, is the core norm of assertion, the expansive norm offers a great alternative to BR, including its compound versions.

3.5.6 Only the Facts? Veracity and Assertion

The expansive sincerity-rule BR" forbids unjustified assertions, and is therefore stronger than the belief-rule BR, which is too lenient. Consequently, it fares better than it, delivering predictions similar to JR. But what if both BR" and JR, despite being stricter than BR, still aren't strict enough? This is a standard accusation against justification-rules, which also applies to the expansive view. For both views, false assertions are perfectly permissible, as long as they are (e.g.) reasonably believed to be true.

Indeed, people share the *intuition* that a false assertion is (ceteris paribus) incorrect and improper. This intuition often translates into action: people typically criticise false assertions in virtue of their being false; falsity itself constitutes a distinctive kind of wrongness for assertions. Both JR and BR" overlook this fundamental linguistic datum.

Factive accounts (KR and TR), by contrast, explain the wrongness and criticisability of false assertions in terms of the infraction of a *factive norm*: since KR and TR forbid making false claims, false assertions are criticisable because they violate the standard set by the norm. This explanation isn't open to non-factive accounts like BR and JR (cf. Williamson 1996, 514), since they don't forbid false assertions.

---

[91] I presented one possible derivation, but other options are available – for example, exploiting the Relevance Principle (Wilson and Sperber 2002), 'questions under discussion' (Roberts 2012), or conversational goals (see the next section).

These considerations bring to light the normative significance of the opposition between expectations of *objective veracity* and *subjective sincerity* (introduced in Section 2.1.4). If proponents of factive accounts are correct, then assertion is subject to a norm of *objective veracity* on top of sincerity: to be epistemically permissible, a statement needs to be true, on top of being sincere. But is this right? Let's focus on non-factive rules that have survived previous scrutiny: JR and BR". These views classify false assertions as improper only when they are disbelieved by the speaker or unjustified. Assertions that are justifiably believed but false (call these UNLUCKY ASSERTIONS for simplicity) are instead deemed appropriate. Is this verdict correct?

If UNLUCKY ASSERTIONS are impermissible in virtue of being false, factive accounts make the right call: objective truth is required for permissible assertion. By contrast, if UNLUCKY ASSERTIONS are permissible in virtue of being reasonably believed to be true, factive accounts are wrong: objective truth isn't required for permissible assertion after all. To test intuitions, let's consider an example (from Marsili and Wiegmann 2021):

> COFFEE
> *Mallory manages an independent coffee shop. One of her customers is interested in the history and culture of coffee.*
>
> *The customer asks Mallory whether the coffee is from Colombia. Mallory checks the coffee beans label, which says that the coffee is indeed from Colombia, so she replies:*
>
> (13) *The coffee is from Colombia.*
>
> *However, Mallory doesn't know that the labels have been mixed up at the factory, and that the coffee beans are actually from Guatemala.*

Mallory here says something false. But what else could have Mallory done? By giving the opposite answer ('The coffee is not from Colombia') Mallory would hit truth purely by chance, at the price of lying. By refusing to answer, she could surely avoid saying something false. But it would not only be rude; it would presumably violate some other communicative and epistemic norms (Goldberg 2020). On the other hand, responding with (13) seems totally appropriate, given what Mallory knows. Accordingly, many philosophers insist that UNLUCKY ASSERTIONS are permissible.

The intuition that Mallory would be making an appropriate assertion is overwhelmingly shared by non-philosophers: a strong majority (about 92 per cent) of speakers disagree with the statement 'Mallory should not have said that the coffee is from Colombia'. Generalising, empirical studies consistently found that laypeople deem unlucky assertions appropriate and permissible

(Kneer 2018, 2021; Reuter and Brössel 2019; Marsili and Wiegmann 2021).[92] Assuming that a good account of the norm of assertion 'must face the linguistic data' (Douven 2006, 450; see also Kneer 2018), and make predictions that are generally consistent with the linguistic intuitions and appraisals of competent speakers, these studies provide strong support for non-factive accounts.[93]

To deny that the norm of assertion is factive is not to deny a link between assertion and truth (nor the importance of veracity for testimony). An essential link with truth can be maintained by arguing that truth is the purported *aim* (or *goal*), rather than the norm, of assertion (Dummett 1973; Williams 2002; Marsili 2018b; 2024). On this view, assertions are akin to other goal-directed activities: just as scoring a goal is the measure of success for a penalty shot in football (but failing to score a goal is not impermissible), truth is the measure of success for assertion (but failing to assert the truth is not *ipso facto* impermissible). An assertion 'scores' and warrants positive evaluation when it represents reality accurately, and is defective (though not necessarily impermissible) when it fails to match the facts. Truth, in short, sets the standard for evaluating the *success* of assertions, not their permissibility.

This view explains why false assertions are intrinsically defective and criticisable, naturally complementing the normative picture predicated by justification-rules and sincerity-rules. If communicating the truth is the purported goal of assertion, it's only natural that our social practice should forbid behaviour that is not conducive to asserting truths – such as making assertions that one doesn't believe to be true, or that aren't supported by adequate evidence. So understood, non-factive rules like BR" promote the achievement of assertion's goal: their function is to maximise the proportion of true assertions. This, in turn, ensures that testimony is generally veridical.

4 Conclusion: The Value of Sincerity

This Element has explained what makes sincerity valuable in our society. It sustains our ability to communicate, to exchange knowledge, and to coordinate

---

[92] Some initial findings by John Turri suggested that the norm of assertion is knowledge. However, every other researcher found incompatible results, and a strong case has now been made against the methodology employed in Turri's pioneering studies (Marsili and Wiegmann 2021; Graham and Pedersen 2024; Kneer and Marsili 2025).

[93] Some factivist philosophers insist that these results are compatible with their view: if unlucky assertions are judged permissible, it is not because they comply with the norm, but rather because they violate it in an excusable way (comparable to the excusable promise-breaking discussed in Section 2.7.2). Apart from facing substantive theoretical objections (Douven 2006, 478–80; Lackey 2007; Gerken 2011; Schechter 2017), this 'excuse manoeuvre' faces empirical evidence that decisively speaks against it. Studies show that laypeople judge that unlucky assertions are plainly permissible, in patterns that deviate from the typical manifestations of excuse validation (Graham and Pedersen 2024; Kneer and Marsili 2025, 90–93).

action, allowing us to form and maintain the complex social relationships that define human life.

Sincerity may appear deceptively simple – you just have to say what you believe. Yet, this apparent simplicity conceals substantial complexity, as we have seen throughout the first half (Section 2) of this Element. Accordingly, a satisfying analysis of the phenomenon has escaped philosophers and linguists for centuries. Reviewing previous attempts led us to make some progress, though. I've argued that the *intentional expression view* resolves puzzles that have plagued speaker-centred accounts since their inception: even when beliefs fragment or speakers misspeak, sincerity tracks what speakers intend to express. Building upon previous work on degrees of sincerity, the notion of *alethic proximity* offers an improved framework for understanding how imprecision and uncertainty affect evaluations of sincerity. Discussion of non-assertoric illocutions, too, has improved upon existing work in speech act theory, delivering a broader, 'unbound' model that extends insincerity to the intentional violation of any felicity condition.

The second half of this Element (Section 3) applied this conceptual toolbox to normative questions. Different conceptions of sincerity translated into different articulations of what sincerity demands, both as a norm and as a virtue. After briefly reviewing sincerity's relation to other norms, its status as a virtue, and its role in supporting valuable social practices, I explored how a norm of sincerity might sustain assertion's epistemic value. The most significant contribution of this part is the *expansive view*, which represents a promising new entry into the landscape of competing norms of assertion, and which revives the once-popular idea that sincerity is all that assertion demands.

The expansive view yields permissibility verdicts similar to the justification-rule, but (unlike compound views) it derives epistemic normativity entirely from expectations of sincerity. Paired with the idea that truth is the aim of assertion, it acknowledges that false assertions are intrinsically defective, while avoiding the problems faced by factive rules (like the knowledge-rule and the truth-rule). Together with justification-rules, it one of offers the most plausible accounts of the epistemic norm of assertion.

Space constraints force me to leave many interesting questions unexplored. Some open threads involve the application of our conceptual repertoire to more complex domains. For example, when multiple speakers with differing beliefs jointly make an assertion as a group, what determines whether they are sincere?[94] Other questions concern the study of sincerity in other areas of philosophy (moral

---

[94] For discussion, see Lackey 2020 and Marsili 2023.

and political philosophy), in other disciplines (psychology, politics, and law), and in other philosophical and cultural traditions (see e.g. Rogacz 2022). Far from resolving all puzzles, this Element offers tools and resources that lend themselves to many uses – not only for academic researchers but for anyone striving to navigate a world where sincerity is the rule, but insincerity is nonetheless commonplace.

References

Adler, Jonathan E. 1997. 'Lying, Deceiving, or Falsely Implicating'. *Journal of Philosophy* 94 (9): 435–52.

Aldrich, Virgil C. 1966. 'Telling, Acknowledging and Asserting'. *Analysis* 27 (2): 53–56.

Alfano, Mark, and Neil Levy. 2020. 'Knowledge from Vice: Deeply Social Epistemology.' *Mind* 129 (515): 887–915. https://doi.org/10.1093/mind/fzz017.

Alston, William P. 2000. *Illocutionary Acts and Sentence Meaning*. Cornell University Press.

Aquinas. ST. *Summa Theologica*. Lulu.com.

Aristotle. NE. *Nicomachean Ethics*. Hackett Publishing.

Artiga, Marc, and Cédric Paternotte. 2018. 'Deception: A Functional Account'. *Philosophical Studies* 175 (3): 579–600. https://doi.org/10.1007/s11098-017-0883-8.

Augustine. DM. *De Mendacio*. CreateSpace Independent Publishing Platform.

Austin, John Langshaw. 1975. *How To Do Things with Words*. 2nd ed. Clarendon Press.

Bach, Kent. 2008. 'Applying Pragmatics to Epistemology'. *Philosophical Issues* 18: 68–88.

Bach, Kent, and Robert M. Harnish. 1979. *Linguistic Communication and Speech Acts*. MIT Press.

Benton, Matthew Aaron. 2018. 'Lying, Accuracy and Credence'. *Analysis* 78 (2): 195–98. https://doi.org/10.1093/analys/anx132.

Bok, Sissela. 1978. *Lying*. Random House.

Carson, Thomas L. 2006. 'The Definition of Lying'. *Noûs* 40 (2): 284–306.

Carson, Thomas L. 2010. *Lying and Deception*. Oxford University Press.

Carson, Thomas L. 2018. 'Lying and Ethics'. In *The Oxford Handbook of Lying*, edited by Jörg Meibauer. Oxford University Press. https://doi.org/10.1093/oxfordhb/9780198736578.013.36.

Carson, Thomas L., Richard E Wokutch, and Kent F Murrmann. 1982. 'Bluffing in Labor Negotiations: Issues Legal and Ethical'. *Journal of Business Ethics* 1 (1): 13–22.

Cassam, Quassim. 2018. 'Epistemic Insouciance'. *Journal of Philosophical Research* 43: 1–20. https://doi.org/10.5840/jpr2018828131.

Chan, Timothy, and Guy Kahane. 2011. 'The Trouble with Being Sincere'. *Canadian Journal of Philosophy* 41 (2): 1–13. www.ncbi.nlm.nih.gov/pmc/articles/pmc3272424/.

Chisholm, Roderick M., and Thomas D Feehan. 1977. 'The Intent to Deceive'. *Journal of Philosophy* 74 (3): 143–59.

Clem, Stewart. 2023. *Lying and Truthfulness: A Thomistic Perspective.* Cambridge University Press. https://doi.org/10.1017/9781009261418.

Coady, Cecil Anthony John. 1992. *Testimony.* Oxford University Press. https://doi.org/10.1093/0198235518.001.0001.

Cohen, Gerald Allan. 2002. 'Deeper into Bullshit'. In *Countours of Agency: Essays on Themes from Harry Frankfurt,* edited by Sarah Buss and Lee Overton. MIT Press. 321–339.

Cullison, Andrew. 2010. 'On the Nature of Testimony'. *Episteme* 7(2):114–27. https://doi.org/10.3366/E1742360010000857.

Curzer, Howard J. 2012. *Aristotle and the Virtues.* Oxford University Press.

Davis, Wayne. 1999. 'Communicating, Telling and Informing'. *Philosophical Inquiry* 21 (1): 21–43.

Davis, Wayne. 2003. *Meaning, Expression and Thought.* Cambridge University Press.

Davis, Wayne. 2010."Implicature", In *The Stanford Encyclopedia of Philosophy* (Spring 2024 Edition), edited by Edward N. Zalta & Uri Nodelman (Eds.) <https://plato.stanford.edu/archives/spr2024/entries/implicature/>.

Douven, Igor. 2006. 'Assertion, Knowledge, and Rational Credibility'. *The Philosophical Review* 115 (4): 449–85. https://doi.org/10.1215/00318108-2006-010.

Dummett, Michael. 1973. 'Assertion'. In *Frege: Philosophy of Language,* edited by Duckworth. pp. 295–363.

Erickson, Thomas D., and Mark E. Mattson. 1981. 'From Words to Meaning: A Semantic Illusion'. *Journal of Verbal Learning and Verbal Behavior* 20 (5): 540–51. https://doi.org/10.1016/S0022-5371(81)90165-1.

Eriksson, John. 2011. 'Straight Talk: Conceptions of Sincerity in Speech'. *Philosophical Studies* 153 (2): 213–34. https://doi.org/10.1007/s11098-009-9487-2.

Falkenberg, Gabriel. 1988. 'Insincerity and Disloyalty'. *Argumentation* 2 (1): 89–97. https://doi.org/10.1007/BF00179143.

Fallis, Don. 2010. 'Lying and Deception'. *Philosophers' Imprint* 10 (11): 1–22.

Fallis, Don. 2012. 'Lying as a Violation of Grice's First Maxim of Quality'. *Dialectica* 66 (4): 563–81. https://doi.org/10.1111/1746-8361.12007.

Fallis, Don. 2018. 'Lying and Omissions'. In *The Oxford Handbook of Lying.* Oxford University Press. pp. 183–92. https://doi.org/10.1093/oxfordhb/9780198736578.013.13.

Fallis, Don, and Peter J. Lewis. 2021. 'Animal Deception and the Content of Signals'. *Studies in History and Philosophy of Science Part A* 87 (June): 114–24. https://doi.org/10.1016/j.shpsa.2021.03.004.

Faulkner, Paul. 2013. 'Lying and Deceit'. In *The International Encyclopedia of Ethics*, edited by H Lafollette. Wiley. http://onlinelibrary.wiley.com/doi/10.1002/9781444367072.wbiee482/full.

Foucault, Michel. 2011. *The Courage of Truth*. 2011th ed. Translated by Graham Burchell. Palgrave Macmillan.

Frankfurt, Harry. 1986. *On Bullshit*. Princeton University Press.

Frege, Gottlob. 1956. 'The Thought: A Logical Inquiry'. In *Mind*, vol. 65. no. 259 (July 1956). Oxford University Press on behalf of Mind Association. pp. 289–311. https://doi.org/10.2307/2251513.

Fricker, Elizabeth. 2012. 'Stating and Insinuating'. *Aristotelian Society Supplementary Volume* 86 (1): 199–215. https://doi.org/10.1111/j.1467-8349.2012.00214.x.

García-Carpintero, Manuel. 2004. 'Assertion and the Semantics of Force-Markers'. In *The Semantics/Pragmatics Distinction*, edited by Claudia Bianchi. CSLI. pp. 133–166.

García-Carpintero, Manuel. 2022. 'How to Understand Rule-Constituted Kinds'. *Review of Philosophy and Psychology* 13 (1): 7–27. https://doi.org/10.1007/s13164-021-00576-z.

Gerken, Mikkel. 2011. 'Warrant and Action'. *Synthese* 178 (3): 529–47. https://doi.org/10.1007/s11229-009-9655-0.

Goldberg, Sanford C. 2011. 'Putting the Norm of Assertion to Work: The Case of Testimony'. In *Assertion: New Philosophical Essays*, edited by Jessica Brown and Herman Cappelen. Oxford University Press. pp. 175–96 *https://doi.org/10.1093/acprof:oso/9780199573004.003.0008*

Goldberg, Sanford C. 2015. *Assertion: On the Philosophical Significance of Assertoric Speech*. Oxford University Press.

Goldberg, Sanford C. 2020. *Conversational Pressure: Normativity in Speech Exchanges*. Oxford University Press.

Graham, Peter J. 2020. 'Assertions, Handicaps, and Social Norms'. *Episteme* 17 (3): 349–63. https://doi.org/10.1017/epi.2019.53.

Graham, Peter J., and Nikolaj J. L. L. Pedersen. 2024. 'Knowledge Is Not Our Norm of Assertion'. In *Contemporary Debates in Epistemology*, 3rd ed., edited by Blake Roeber, John Turri, Matthias Steup, and Ernest Sosa. Routledge. pp. 339–354.

Green, Mitchell. 2007. *Self-Expression*. Oxford University Press. https://doi.org/10.1111/j.1467-9213.2009.618_7.x.

Green, Stuart P. 2018. 'Lying and the Law'. In *The Oxford Handbook of Lying*, edited by Jörg Meibauer. Oxford University Press. pp. 483–94. https://doi .org/10.1093/oxfordhb/9780198736578.013.38.

Grice, Herbert. Paul. 1989. *Studies in the Way of Words*. Harvard University Press.

Griffiths, Paul J. 2004. *Lying: An Augustinian Theology of Duplicity*. Brazos Press.

Güngör, Hüseyin. 2024. 'Non-Literal Lies Are Not Exculpatory'. *The Philosophical Quarterly*, 11 July, pqae078. https://doi.org/10.1093/pq/ pqae078.

Hindriks, Frank. 2007. 'The Status of the Knowledge Account of Assertion'. *Linguistics and Philosophy* 30 (3): 393–406. https://doi.org/10.1007/s10988-007-9019-5.

Heffer, Chris. 2020. *'All Bullshit and Lies?: Insincerity, Irresponsibility, and the Judgment of Untruthfulness'*. Oxford University Press.

Hoek, Daniel. 2018. 'Conversational Exculpature'. *Philosophical Review* 127 (2): 151–96. https://doi.org/10.1215/00318108-4326594.

Holton, Richard. 2008. 'Partial Belief, Partial Intention'. *Mind* 117 (465): 27–58. https://doi.org/10.1093/mind/fzn002.

Hughes, Nick. 2017. 'No Excuses: Against the Knowledge Norm of Belief'. *Thought: A Journal of Philosophy*, ahead of print, 21 July. https://doi.org/ 10.1002/tht3.244.

Isenberg, Arnold. 1964. 'Deontology and the Ethics of Lying'. *Philosophy and Phenomenological Research* 24 (4): 463–80.

Kant, Immanuel. 1797. *On a Supposed Right to Lie Because of Philantropic Concerns*.

Kant, Immanuel. LE. *Lectures on Ethics*. Edited by Peter Heath and Jerome. Borges. Schneewind. Translated by Peter Heath. The Cambridge Edition of the Works of Immanuel Kant. Cambridge University Press. https://doi.org/ 10.1017/CBO9781107049512.

Kneer, Markus. 2018. 'The Norm of Assertion: Empirical Data'. *Cognition* 177: 165–71. https://doi.org/10.1016/j.cognition.2018.03.020.

Kneer, Markus. 2021. 'Norms of Assertion in the United States, Germany, and Japan'. *PNAS* 118 (37): 3.

Klieber, Anna. 2024. 'Conversational Silence, Reconsidered'. *Theoria* 90 (6): 652–68 https://doi.org/10.1111/theo.12566.

Kneer, Markus, and Neri Marsili. 2025. 'The Truth about Assertion and Retraction: A Review of the Empirical Literature'. In *Lying, Fake News, and Bullshit*, edited by Alex Wiegmann. Bloomsbury. pp. 81–116.

Korsgaard, Christine M. 1986. 'The Right to Lie: Kant on Dealing with Evil'. *Philosophy and Public Affairs* 15 (4): 325–49. https://doi.org/10.2307/2265252.

Krauss, Sam Fox. 2017. 'Lying, Risk and Accuracy'. *Analysis* 73: 651–59. https://doi.org/10.1093/analys/anx105.

Krstić, Vladimir. 2019. 'Can You Lie without Intending to Deceive?' *Pacific Philosophical Quarterly* 100 (2): 642–60. https://doi.org/10.1111/papq.12241.

Krstić, Vladimir. 2023. 'Lying: Revisiting the "Intending to Deceive" Condition'. *Analysis* 83 (2): 249–59. https://doi.org/10.1093/analys/anac099.

Krstić, Vladimir. 2025. *Deception and Self-Deception: A Unified Account.* Cambridge University Press. www.cambridge.org/core/elements/deception-and-selfdeception/F245F27D1A823DB21CC24B9C2D161C7A.

Lackey, Jennifer. 2006. 'The Nature of Testimony'. *Pacific Philosophical Quarterly* 87 (2): 177–97. https://doi.org/10.1111/j.1468-0114.2006.00254.x.

Lackey, Jennifer. 2007. 'Norms of Assertion'. *Noûs* 41 (4): 594–626. https://doi.org/10.1111/j.1747-9991.2007.00065.x.

Lackey, Jennifer. 2020. *The Epistemology of Groups.* Oxford University Press.

Lasersohn, Peter. 1999. 'Pragmatic Halos'. *Language.* 75(3): 522–51.

Leonard, Nick. 2023. 'Epistemological Problems of Testimony'. In *The Stanford Encyclopedia of Philosophy*, Spring 2023, edited by Edward N. Zalta and Uri Nodelman. Metaphysics Research Lab, Stanford University. https://plato.stanford.edu/archives/spr2023/entriesestimony-epis prob/.

Lewis, David K. 1975. 'Languages and Language'. In *Minnesota Studies in the Philosophy of Science*, edited by Keith Gunderson. University of Minnesota Press. pp. 3–35.

Mahon, James Edwin. 2006. 'Kant and the Perfect Duty to Others Not to Lie'. *British Journal for the History of Philosophy* 14 (4): 653–85. https://doi.org/10.1080/09608780600956407.

Mahon, James Edwin. 2015. 'The Definition of Lying and Deception'. In *Stanford Encyclopedia of Philosophy.* (Winter 2016 Edition),edited by Edward N. Zalta, Metaphysics Research Lab, Stanford University. URL = <https://plato.stanford.edu/archives/win2016/entries/lying-

Mandelkern, Matthew, and Kevin Dorst. 2022. 'Assertion Is Weak'. *Philosophers' Imprint*, ahead of print. https://doi.org/10.3998/phimp.1076.

Marsili, Neri. 2014. 'Lying as a Scalar Phenomenon'. In *Certainty-Uncertainty – and the Attitudinal Space in Between*, edited by Sibilla Cantarini, Werner Abraham, and Elisabeth Leiss. John Benjamins Publishing Company. pp. 153–73. https://doi.org/10.1075/slcs.165.09mar.

Marsili, Neri. 2016. 'Lying by Promising'. *International Review of Pragmatics* 8 (2): 271–313. https://doi.org/10.1163/18773109-00802005.

Marsili, Neri. 2017. 'You Don't Say! Lying, Asserting and Insincerity'. July. PhD Dissertation, University of Sheffield. https://etheses.whiterose.ac.uk/19068/.

Marsili, Neri. 2018a. 'Lying and Certainty'. In *The Oxford Handbook of Lying*, edited by Jörg Meibauer. Oxford University Press. pp. 170–82. https://doi.org/10.1093/oxfordhb/9780198736578.013.12.

Marsili, Neri. 2018b. 'Truth and Assertion: Rules versus Aims'. *Analysis* 78 (4): 638–48. https://doi.org/10.1093/analys/any008.

Marsili, Neri, Eliot Michaelson and Andreas Stokke (Eds.). 2021a. 'Lying: Language, Knowledge, Ethics, and Politics (Oxford: Oxford University Press, 2018), Pp. 320.' *Utilitas* 33 (4): 502–5. https://doi.org/10.1017/S0953820821000182.

Marsili, Neri. 2021b. 'Lying, Speech Acts, and Commitment'. *Synthese* 199: 3245–69. https://doi.org/10.1007/s11229-020-02933-4.

Marsili, Neri. 2022. 'Immoral Lies and Partial Beliefs'. *Inquiry* 65 (1): 117–27. https://doi.org/10.1080/0020174X.2019.1667865.

Marsili, Neri. 2023a. 'Group Assertions and Group Lies'. *Topoi* 42 (2): 369–84. https://doi.org/10.1007/s11245-022-09875-1.

Marsili, Neri. 2023b. 'Towards a Unified Theory of Illocutionary Normativity'. In *Sbisà on Speech as Action*, edited by Laura Caponetto and Paolo Labinaz. Palgrave Macmillan. pp. 165–94.

Marsili, Neri. 2024. 'Truth: The Rule or the Aim of Assertion?' *Episteme* 21 (1): 263–69. https://doi.org/10.1017/epi.2021.28.

Marsili, Neri. (forthcoming) . 'How Online Misinformation Works: A Costly Signalling Perspective'. In *Misinformation and Other Epistemic Pathologies.*, edited by Mihaela Popa-Wyatt. Cambridge University Press.

Marsili, Neri, and Alex Wiegmann. 2021. 'Should I Say That? An Experimental Investigation of the Norm of Assertion.' *Cognition* 212. https://doi.org/10.1016/j.cognition.2021.104657.

Marsili, Neri, and Guido Löhr. 2022. 'Saying, Commitment, and the Lying-Misleading Distinction'. *The Journal of Philosophy* 119 (12): 687–98. https://doi.org/10.5840/jphil20221191243.

Marsili, Neri, and Mitchell Green. 2021. 'Assertion: A (Partly) Social Speech Act'. *Journal of Pragmatics* 181 (August): 17–28. https://doi.org/10.1016/j.pragma.2021.03.016.

McGlynn, Aidan. 2014. *Knowledge First?* Palgrave Macmillan.

Meibauer, Jörg. 2005. 'Lying and Falsely Implicating'. *Journal of Pragmatics* 37 (9): 1373–99. https://doi.org/10.1016/j.pragma.2004.12.007.

Meibauer, Jörg. 2014. *Lying at the Semantics-Pragmatics Interface*. De Gruyter. https://doi.org/10.1515/9781614510840.

Mellor, David. Hugh. 1977. 'Conscious Belief'. *Proceedings of the Aristotelian Society* 78: 87–101. www.jstor.org/stable/4544919.

Milić, Ivan. 2017. 'Against Selfless Assertions'. *Philosophical Studies* 174 (9): 2277–95. https://doi.org/10.1007/s11098-016-0798-9.

Miller, Christian B. 2021. *Honesty: The Philosophy and Psychology of a Neglected Virtue*. Oxford University Press.

Millikan, Ruth Garrett. 2005. *Language: A Biological Model*. no. 118. Oxford: Clarendon Press.

Moran, Richard. 2005. 'Problems of Sincerity'. *Proceedings of the Aristotelian Society* 105 (1): 325–45. https://doi.org/10.1111/j.0066-7373.2004.00117.x.

Nagel, Thomas. 1998. 'Concealment and Exposure'. *Philosophy & Public Affairs* 27 (1): 3–30. https://doi.org/10.1111/j.1088-4963.1998.tb00057.x.

Owens, David. 2006. 'Testimony and Assertion'. *Philosophical Studies* 130 (1): 105–29. https://doi.org/10.1007/s11098-005-3237-x.

Pagin, Peter, and Neri Marsili. 2021. 'Assertion'. In *Stanford Encyclopedia of Philosophy*, Winter 2021 ed., edited by Edward N. Zalta. https://plato.stanford.edu/archives/win2021/entries/assertion/.

Pennycook, Gordon, James Allan Cheyne, Nathaniel Barr, Derek J Koehler, and Jonathan A Fugelsang. 2015. 'On the Reception and Detection of Pseudo-Profound Bullshit'. *Judgment and Decision Making* 10 (6): 549–63. https://doi.org/10.3389/fpsyg.2013.00279.

Pepp, Jessica. 2018. 'Truth Serum, Liar Serum, and Some Problems about Saying What You Think Is False'. In *Lying: Language, Knowledge, Ethics, Politics*, edited by Eliot Michaelson & Andeas Stokke (Eds.), Oxford University Press. pp. 43–64.

Pepp, Jessica. 2024. 'The Size of a Lie: From Truthlikeness to Sincerity'. *Inquiry*: 1–24. https://doi.org/10.1080/0020174X.2024.2376350.

Pinker, Steven, Martin A. Nowak, and James J. Lee. 2008. 'The Logic of Indirect Speech'. *Proceedings of the National Academy of Sciences of the United States of America* 105 (3): 833–38. https://doi.org/10.1073/pnas.0707192105.

Queloz, Matthieu. 2021. *The Practical Origins of Ideas: Genealogy as Conceptual Reverse-Engineering*. 1st ed. Oxford University Press. https://doi.org/10.1093/oso/9780198868705.001.0001.

Reuter, Kevin, and Peter Brössel. 2019. 'No Knowledge Required'. *Episteme* 16 (3): 303–21. https://doi.org/10.1017/epi.2018.10.

Ridge, Michael. 2006. 'Sincerity and Expressivism'. *Philosophical Studies* 131 (2): 487–510. https://doi.org/10.1007/s.

Roberts, Craige. 2012. 'Information Structure in Discourse: Towards an Integrated Formal Theory of Pragmatics'. *Semantics and Pragmatics* 5 (6): 1–69. https://doi.org/10.3765/sp.5.6.

Rogacz, Dawid. 2022. 'Sincerity (Cheng) as a Civic and Political Virtue in Classical Confucian Philosophy'. *Philosophy Compass* 17 (6): e12833. https://doi.org/10.1111/phc3.12833.

Rosch, Eleanor. 1973. 'On the Internal Structure of Perceptual and Semantic Categories'. In *Cognitive Development and the Acquisition of Language*, edited by T. E. Moore. Academic Press. pp. 111–44. https://doi.org/10.1016/B978-0-12-505850-6.50010-4.

Rousseau, Jean-Jacques. RSW. *The Reveries of the Solitary Walker*. Hackett Publishing.

Russell, Bertrand. 1946. *History of Western Philosophy*. Routledge.

Rutschmann, Ronja, and Alex Wiegmann. 2017. 'No Need for an Intention to Deceive? Challenging the Traditional Definition of Lying'. *Philosophical Psychology* 30 (4): 438–57. https://doi.org/10.1080/09515089.2016.1277382.

Saul, Jennifer M. 2012. *Lying, Misleading, and What Is Said: An Exploration in Philosophy of Language and Ethics*. no. 1. Oxford University Press.

Saul, Jennifer M. 2024. *Dogwhistles and Figleaves: How Manipulative Language Spreads Racism and Falsehood*. Oxford University Press.

Schechter, Joshua. 2017. 'No Need for Excuses against Knowledge-First Epistemology and the Knowledge Norm of Assertion'. In *Knowledge First: Approaches in Epistemology and Mind*, edited by J. Adam Carter, Emma C. Gordon, and Benjamin W. Jarvis. Oxford University Press. pp. 132–60. https://doi.org/10.1093/oso/9780198716310.003.0007.

Schiffer, Stephen R. 1972. *Meaning*. Clarendon Press.

Searcy, William, and Stephen Nowicki. 2005. *The Evolution of Animal Communication: Reliability and Deception in Signaling Systems*. Princeton University Press.

Searle, John R. 1969. *Speech Acts: An Essay in the Philosophy of Language*. Cambridge University Press.

Searle, John R. 1979. *Expression and Meaning*. Cambridge University Press.

Sedgwick, Sally. 1991. 'On Lying and the Role of Content in Kant's Ethics'. *Kant-Studien* 82 (1): 42–62. https://doi.org/10.1515/kant.1991.82.1.42.

Siebel, M. 2003. Illocutionary Acts and Attitude Expression. *Linguistics and Philosophy* 26, 351–66. https://doi.org/10.1023/A:1024110814662.

Siebel, Mark. 2020. 'The Belief View of Assertion'. *The Oxford Handbook of Assertion*: 98–118. https://doi.org/10.1093/oxfordhb/9780190675233.013.4.

Siegler, Frederick A. 1966. 'Lying'. *American Philosophical Quarterly* 3 (2): 128–36.

Simion, Mona. 2018. 'Saying and Believing: The Norm Commonality Assumption'. *Philosophical Studies*, ahead of print. https://doi.org/10.1007/s11098-018-1105-8.

Skyrms, Brian. 2010. *Signals: Evolution, Learning, & Information*. Oxford University Press.

Smith, John Maynard, and David Harper. 2003. *Animal Signals*. Oxford Series in Ecology and Evolution. Oxford University Press.

Sneddon, Andrew. 2021. Alternative Motivation and Lies'. *Analysis* 81 (1): 46–52. https://doi.org/10.1093/analys/anaa027.

Sorensen, Roy. 2007. 'Bald-Faced Lies! Lying without the Intent to Deceive'. *Pacific Philosophical Quarterly* 88: 251–64. http://onlinelibrary.wiley.com/doi/10.1111/j.1468-0114.2007.00290.x/full.

Sorensen, Roy. 2010. 'Knowledge-Lies'. *Analysis* 70 (4): 608–15. https://doi.org/10.1093/analys/anq072.

Sorensen, Roy. 2011. 'What Lies behind Misspeaking'. *American Philosophical Quarterly* 48 (4): 399–410.

Sorensen, Roy. 2018. 'Lying to Mindless Machines'. In *Lying: Language, Knowledge, Ethics, Politics*, edited by Eliot Michaelson and Andreas Stokke. Oxford University Press. pp. 285–97. https://doi.org/10.1093/oso/9780198743965.001.0001.

Sorensen, Roy. 2023. 'Vagueness'. In *The Stanford Encyclopedia of Philosophy*, Winter 2023, edited by Edward N. Zalta and Uri Nodelman. Metaphysics Research Lab, Stanford University. https://plato.stanford.edu/archives/win2023/entries/vagueness/.

Sperber, Dan, Fabrice Clement, Christophe Heintz, et al. 2010. 'Epistemic Vigilance'. *Mind and Language* 25 (4): 359–93. https://doi.org/10.1111/j.1468-0017.2010.01394.x.

Stenius, Erik. 1967. 'Mood and Language-Game'. *Synthese* 17 (3): 254–74. www.jstor.org/stable/20114558.

Stokke, Andreas. 2017. 'Lies, Harm, and Practical Interests'. *Philosophy and Phenomenological Research* 2007: 1–17. https://doi.org/10.1111/phpr.12439.

Stokke, Andreas. 2018. *Lying and Insincerity*. Oxford University Press.

Strawson, Peter Frederick. 1964. 'Intention and Convention in Speech Acts'. *The Philosophical Review* 73 (4): 439–60.

Strudler, Alan. 2009. 'The Distinctive Wrong in Lying'. *Ethical Theory and Moral Practice* 13 (2): 171–79. https://doi.org/10.1007/s10677-009-9194-2.

Swift, Jonathan. 1710. *The Art Of Political Lying*. http://archive.org/details/swift-the-art-of-political-lying-1710.

Tagliapietra, Andrea. 2003. *La virtú crudele. Filosofia e storia della sincerità*. Einaudi.

Trilling, Lionel. 2009. *Sincerity and Authenticity*. Harvard University Press.

Turri, John. 2014. 'Selfless Assertions: Some Empirical Evidence'. *Synthese* 192: 1221–23. https://doi.org/10.1007/s11229-014-0621-0.

Varga, Somogy, and Charles Guignon. 2023. 'Authenticity'. In *The Stanford Encyclopedia of Philosophy*, Summer 2023, edited by Edward N. Zalta and Uri Nodelman. Metaphysics Research Lab, Stanford University. https://plato.stanford.edu/archives/sum2023/entries/authenticity/.

Viebahn, Emanuel. 2017. 'Non-Literal Lies'. *Erkenntnis* 82: 1367–80. https://doi.org/10.1007/s10670-017-9880-8.

Viebahn, Emanuel. 2021. 'The Lying/Misleading Distinction: A Commitment-Based Approach'. *Journal of Philosophy* CXVIII 6: 289–319.

Weiner, Matthew. 2005. 'Must We Know What We Say?' *The Philosophical Review* 114 (2): 227–51. https://doi.org/10.1215/00318108-114-2-227.

Whiting, Daniel. 2012. 'Stick to the Facts: On the Norms of Assertion'. *Erkenntnis* 78 (4): 847–67. https://doi.org/10.1007/s10670-012-9383-6.

Williams, Bernard Arthur Owen. 2002. *Truth and Truthfulness an Essay in Genealogy*. Princeton University Press.

Williamson, Timothy. 1996. 'Knowing and Asserting'. *The Philosophical Review* 105 (4): 489–523.

Wilson, Deirdre. 1995. 'Is There a Maxim of Truthfulness'. *UCL Working Papers in Linguistics* 7: 197–212.

Wilson, Deirdre, and Dan Sperber. 2002. 'Truthfulness and Relevance'. *Mind* 25: 1–41.

Acknowledgements

I am grateful to Mark Alfano, Emma Bolton, Michel Croce, Ivan Milić, Christian Miller, Jessica Pepp, Andreas Stokke, and two anonymous referees for their helpful comments on earlier versions of this manuscript. This work was supported by an 'Attracción de Talento' grant funded by the Community of Madrid (grant number: 2022-T1/HUM-24071) and by the European Research Council (ERC) under the European Union's Horizon Europe research and innovation programme (Grant agreement No. 101164219).

For EU product safety concerns, contact us at Calle de José Abascal, 56–1°,
28003 Madrid, Spain or eugpsr@cambridge.org.